Architectural Follies in America

GWYN HEADLEY

PRESERVATION
PRESS

JOHN WILEY & SONS, INC.
New York · Chichester · Brisbane · Toronto · Singapore

This text is printed on acid-free paper.

Copyright © 1996 by Gwyn Headley

Published by John Wiley & Sons, Inc.

All rights reserved. Published simultaneously in Canada

Reproduction or translation of any part of this work beyond that permitted by section 107 or 108 of the United States Copyright Act without the permission of the copyright owner is unlawful. Requests for permission or further information should be addressed to the Permissions Department, John Wiley & Sons, Inc., 605 Third Avenue, New York, NY 10158-0012.

This publication is designed to provide accurate and authoritative information in regard to the subject matter covered. It is sold with the understanding that the publisher is not engaged in rendering legal, accounting, or other professional services. If legal advice or other expert assistance is required, the services of a competent professional person should be sought.

Library of Congress Cataloging in Publication Data:
Headley, Gwyn.
    Architectural follies in America / Gwyn Headley.
        p   cm.
    ISBN 0-471-14362-6 (paper)
    1. Follies (Architecture)—United States. 2. Grotesque in architecture—United States. 3. Architecture, Modern—United States. I. Title.
    NA208.5.H43 1996
    720'.973—dc20   95-46176
                                                            CIP

Printed in the United States of America

10 9 8 7 6 5 4 3 2 1

For Mike Shatzkin, Thom Tessier, and Donna Wilkinson.
Real Americans.

CONTENTS

ACKNOWLEDGMENTS

This book was decrassified by Yvonne Seeley to whom, as always, much love and many thanks.

In Arizona: Tom and Minamarie Crane, Matt Bianco

In California: "Skipper," Alisa Austin, Carol C. Proctor, Caroline O'Connell, Chris Nichols, Colin P. Flaherty, David Perceval, Donald A. Leonard, Dr. Paul Rich, Frances Butler, Ginger Mallette, Kristy White, Lorraine Forestiere, Mitchell S. Logsdon, Roger B. Taylor, Susan Subtle, Tiffany Reuter

In Connecticut: Thom and Alice Tessier, Joe Vallenino, Denis Jones, Dr. David Poirier

In the District of Columbia: Ivars Gutmanis, Buckley Jeppson

In Florida: Susan Marger, Mary Lou Jansen, Marilyn Kirby, Vita Henshaw, Clell Villella, Howard S. Solomon, Jill Chamberlin

In Illinois: Terry and Barbara Healy

In Louisiana: Sarah Dunbar, Lan Sluder, Brian Comeaux, Carl Brasseaux

In Maine: Ric Jorgensen

In Massachusetts: R. A. Horne

In Montana: Mark Hufstetler

In Nevada: Brad Wiley, Ellen and Clint

In New York: Eve Kahn, Richard Margolis, Alan Burdick, Andrew Alpern, Sue Daglian, Jane Gelfman, Kathleen Mahoney, David

Masello, Fred McCormack, Martha Moran, Randy Reed, Connie Sayre, Mike Shatzkin, Larry Silver, Daniel Waldron, Donna Wilkinson, Nancy Sweetser, Mark Orwell

In Ohio: Theodore Gantz, Charles Fleischmann, Jan Weigel

In Pennsylvania: James Biddle, Jill McConkey

In Rhode Island: Kelly Moran, Debbie Wiley

In Washington: Patricia Watkinson

In Great Britain: Yvonne Seeley, Tess Canfield, Dianne Coles, Michael Cousins, Honor Godfrey, Lucinda Lambton, Justine Oliver, Diana Reynell, Vivienne Schuster, Andrew Plumridge, Belinda Eade

In the Netherlands: Wim Meulenkamp, Pieter and Rita Boogaart, Frances Staatsen

INTRODUCTION

ere is the only sentence in this book that will mention
Florenz Ziegfeld or Stephen Sondheim. The follies
dealt with here are on the far side of building—structures that are not ordinary buildings but are edifices
that transcend the banal, the commonplace, the simply utilitarian.
These are constructions of character dignified by the name of *folly*.
It is an exclusive, elite club. Not every curious building will qualify,
yet gardens can merit being called follies if their architecture surpasses their horticulture. Architectural follies transcend barriers of
style, time, taste, and nationality. They spring from those most
human of emotions: vanity, pride, passion, and obsession.

It is easier to define what a folly is not, rather than what it is. To
begin with, you cannot consciously build a folly. You will construct
a building for your own reasons, but only other people may call it
folly. The "follies" advertised for sale in the back of glamorous garden magazines are not follies, they are garden buildings—buildings
with fine and honorable pedigrees no doubt, but garden buildings
nevertheless.

Nor can the delightful roadside buildings shaped like ducks,
geese, donuts, burgers, hats, whales, ships, dinosaurs, hot dogs, or
shoes really be called follies. They are billboard architecture, and the
essence of such architecture is to attract attention, to make money;
it is the antithesis of folly. Follies come from peace and content-
ment, or passion and commitment. They come from a surplus of
money, rather than the need to make money. Yet because of the
sheer curiosity and vivacity of many of these billboard buildings, we

cannot pass them by unnoticed. It's a wonderful and almost unique-ly American tradition that rightly deserves a chapter in this book, but these buildings are not follies. They spring from sound commercial motives.

No, follies are not sound. Nor are they commercial. They are motiveless yet motivated. They come from long ago and far away, and tomorrow and right next door. Why should we have to travel 4,656 miles to see the Leaning Tower of Pisa? Why not see it down the block? As, of course, we do, if we live in Niles, Illinois. Why make a pilgrimage to Lourdes in France to effect a miracle cure? There is a perfectly serviceable replica of the grotto at Lourdes in Emmits-burg, Maryland. Why shouldn't our houses all have eight sides? You see, Orson Squire Fowler had a theory . . .

Follies stem from passion, obsession, suspicion. They also come from happiness, grief, and confusion. They can take any form, any style. A folly is a state of mind, not an architectural style. Follies can even have a use or purpose, whether that was in the creator's mind or not.

Building follies was not a fashion imported from Europe. True, the eighteenth-century American gentleman adorned his landscape with little temples, gazebos, and summerhouses inspired by his Eng-lish cousins, but here again these were garden buildings rather than follies. Their construction was never undertaken with the silent concentration of the true folly builder. American follies are nobody's borrowed ideas. They are originals, even when they mimic Old World models. Yet one similarity between the continents is apparent: the reluctance of establishment architectural historians to involve themselves too closely with the type, for it is a minefield for the ambitious academic. The properly trained architectural histori-an needs to verify the context and category of buildings, to know where they stand in the order of things. Follies, however, are riotous and undisciplined, seductive and irrational. They are going to cause problems. Architectural historians need to know dates to place buildings in stylistic context, and they need to know the architect in order to place the work in his chronological résumé. Follies do not provide milestones or landmarks in personal development. These are one-hit wonders.

There are as many reasons for building follies as there are follies. To build a dream house, refusing to realize there will never be suffi-cient funds or time to finish it; to rush headlong into a great venture, building a vast warehouse without goods to fill it; to erect a tower,

ARCHITECTURAL FOLLIES IN AMERICA

simply in the hope that bats will come there to roost; to construct a castle to call a lover to a new and alien land—there lies the passion of the folly builder. This book celebrates that passion. There is—or there should be—a little bit of folly in every building, just as we should admit to a touch of madness in all of us, to balance our sanity. And if there could ever be such a creature as a typical folly builder (for follies by their nature are atypical) he might be a successful retired craftsman or manual worker, physically strong and energetic, accustomed to getting things done his own way, self-reliant, ambitious, artistic although probably unaware of it, one who has difficulty in delegating. You will meet men like this throughout this book: the Joe Valleninos, the George Bournes, the Charlie Yeltons. This is indeed a type who could just as well have been drawn to angling as architecture but who chose, to our lasting gratitude, to bequeath us their thoughts, hopes, and desires in concrete, wood, and stone.

Context is not the language of folly. Follies are out of place and out of time, introspective, extroverted, timid, and bold. Each is a one-of-a-kind, individual work of art forming no part of any chronological or stylistic family. Yet some order has to be imposed so that they can be presented to you. The follies presented here have moved far beyond the simple incomprehension that, in former times, led us sneeringly to label them follies. We should respect them, for there is more humanity to be found in folly than in a century of common sense.

The word *folly* began as a derogatory term, reflecting our ignorance rather than that of the builder. As we will see, many of the wild and wonderful buildings in this book had sound reasons for their construction; reasons that may not seem obvious to us from our insulated, air-conditioned, late twentieth-century viewpoint. It is far better to speak to the people who build them. We heard a rumor of a man living in a barrel on the beach in California: "Agnole's Barrel." When we finally tracked this latter-day Diogenes down to Stinson Beach in Marin County, we discovered a courtly and distinguished architect, Valentino Agnoli, who had designed and built a number of refined houses in the hills above the sea, the roofline of one of which may have borne a passing resemblance to a barrel, and another in Bolinas, right on top of the San Andreas fault, which looked a little like a mushroom. Agnoli's houses are not conventional frame houses, but that does not make them follies.

Mere lack of functionality is not a criterion. If one commissions a famous architect, one is forced to assume, at least in part, the role

These houses are hardly humdrum, but they're not quite follies, either. Above, Agnoli's "barrel house"; below, a mushroom sprouts atop the San Andreas fault.

Architectural Follies in America

of guinea pig. Great architects will not be distracted by the humdrum banalities of daily life. The dean of Florida Southern College in Lakeland complained to Frank Lloyd Wright that rain leaked through the roof onto his desk. "Move your desk," came the terse reply. No, a building does not become a folly simply because it manifestly fails to fulfill its function. There is more to it than that. It is not always the structure as built; it is often the mind of the builder that allows us to honor a structure as a folly.

Take memorials and monuments. There is a natural desire to commemorate a great life or a tragic event; monuments to good news are much rarer. But when the architecture of the monument overwhelms the original sentiment or occasion, then it can be deemed worthy of inclusion here.

Now consider scavenger architecture. The need for shelter is paramount, and houses can be and have been built from every sort of material. Yet in the most extreme cases of scavenger architecture the peculiar materials used have been flaunted like trophies: "Look at me and see what I have done with such unpromising material!" The presentation and design of these scrap shacks often prove that the material itself gave pleasure to the builder, challenging him to think in new and different ways, to solve new problems. Step into a greenhouse on a sunny day and you will immediately understand the problems beginning to face someone who decided to build a house out of glass bottles at the entrance to Death Valley. Here, form follows necessity rather than function.

A correspondent in Boston who builds follies for a hobby pointed out that to an American, nonfunctional architecture is an oxymoron. "The word folly is a nasty condemnation by the neighbors of anything showy, costly, or nonconforming. In small New England towns if you paint your house any color scheme except white clapboards and dark green shutters you run the risk of being accused of having created a 'folly.'" A friend in New York agreed. "There are only two American follies," he asserted, "Fulton's Folly and Seward's Folly. Neither are buildings; one was the first steamboat to sail up the Hudson, the other is Alaska." A glance through this book may surprise my friends. America is crammed with follies, and this introductory work can only skim the surface. There are hundreds more out there waiting to be discovered, and I would like to hear of them.

Chapter 1

CLOUD-CAPP'D TOWERS

The tower is one of the essential folly forms. Naturally the world's first folly was the Tower of Babel, while in front of the great temple of Ramses III at Medinet Habu in Luxor, Egypt, stands a structure built in 1200 B.C., in the alien shape of an Assyrian watchtower, useless in its context but perhaps erected as a triumphal record of a victory over a forgotten foe. There are many reasons for wanting to build towers, but we will gloss over most of them and announce a simple, primary reason: to see and be seen. A tower usually provides a viewing platform, and is hence known as a prospect tower. It also makes an eye-catching landmark or monument. Sometimes it fails on both counts, as does the octagonal Gothic prospect tower at Glenelg in rural Maryland, buried in trees that have grown up around and above it. This is a classic folly tower—a rare find in America—following the old European tradition. The American tradition, however, is never wholly flippant and the country's grim pioneering economy manifested itself in later years as improbable practicality. Towers may have been built as observatories, but why not include a water tank or a set of bells or have it provide some other useful function? If one building can be used for two or more purposes, that's just dandy.

The Glenelg tower was built out of local fieldstone, probably by George Lowndes in the early 1830s, as a belvedere looking south from the Gothic Revival house of Glenelg Manor. The house is now the Glenelg County School, and the tower stands on the edge of the parking lot, shyly peeping out of the wood. The back of the tower is severely plain, nothing but a white wooden door and, far above, a wheel window almost lost in the high wall. The stone is clean and

well dressed, the paint fresh and white. All changes round the other side. An iron chimney pipe juts awkwardly from one wall. Another wheel window on the second floor matches the one at the back, while underneath there are two Gothic-style lancet windows, dusty and broken, with pipes snaking out. The windows look blindly out into a bank of saplings and undergrowth, the once splendid view of Maryland farmland now long obscured.

ARCHITECTURAL FOLLIES IN AMERICA

Views are the essence of prospect towers. There is nothing impractical or mad about wanting to appreciate a view. *Bellevue, belvedere, bellavista,* and *boa vista* show we have French, Italian, Spanish, and Portuguese appreciation of great panoramas. What drives the tower builder? What force impels people to rise above their surroundings, to look out, to look over? Every tower has a use, yet it has always been one of the most popular motifs for the folly builder. Let's think of some possible everyday uses for towers: (1) to observe (enemies, fires, etc.); (2) to enjoy the view; (3) to drop lead shot; (4) to carry noxious by-products into the atmosphere; (5) to uplift the soul; (6) to hang bells in; (7) to create an impression; or (8) to hold a water tank and provide pressure.

This lovely windmill in Chesterton, England, was either copied by Benedict Arnold or—the immeasurably more exciting theory—was itself the copy of a fourteenth-century Norse church in Rhode Island.

One of the greatest architectural arguments in America raged for years over a short and ancient tower in Newport, Rhode Island. Was it built by Governor Benedict Arnold as a windmill in the mid-seventeenth century, or was it built as a fortified church by itinerant Norsemen in the fourteenth century? The latter and immeasurably more exciting theory is dented by the fact that no mention of the curiosity had been made before Arnold described it in his will of 1677 as "my Stone built wind-miln." Early settlers would doubtless already have remarked on such an extraordinary structure, a circular tower standing on eight round-headed arches. But a final blow to the Nordic argument must come from the existence of an otherwise unique stone-built windmill dated 1632 in Chesterton, England, attributed to the great architect Inigo Jones. Apart from the quality of workmanship and state of preservation, the latter tower is all but identical to its American cousin. It is said that two copies of this tower were built in the nineteenth century, but we have yet to find them.

The skeletal octagonal edifice that stands on top of a hill in Marcus Garvey Park, Manhattan, was built in 1856 by Julius Kroehl for the local volunteer fire department. The bell in the middle was cast in Holland in 1633 and came to America in 1656. It has not been rung nor the tower used for observing fires since 1874 yet, somehow, through three name changes for the park and all other odds it has survived unclothed.

The Old Water Tower in Chicago, a delightful nineteenth-century surprise in the city that defines twentieth-century architecture, is fully clothed. It is one of the few buildings to have survived the Great Fire of 1872, and its continued presence is to be applauded. It draws an involuntary gasp of admiration at first sight, packed among titanic towers of smaller wit, a Rapunzel among mammon. It had its use,

Fire and water: Above left, this skeletal fire-observing tower surveys a Manhattan park; above right, Fresno's water tower includes rooms originally meant to house the city's library; right, the Lawson Water Tower looks like a refugee from medieval France.

although one could argue that it was over-architectured for its purpose, but that was a frequent failing among water towers. The basic premise is a tank raised on struts to provide adequate water pressure; once that function is fulfilled anything can happen. The nation rallied round Chicago after the fire. People sent books from all over the country to restock the library that had been lost; even Queen Victoria sent some over from England. But the books arrived before there was any place to put them, so until the new library was built they were stored in the water tower. Thus, when Chicago architect George S. Mayer was commissioned by the young city of Fresno, California, to design a new water tower in 1894, he assumed that all water towers had libraries in their bases and built one on the second and third levels of the Fresno water tower. But the city didn't have enough books to fill it, so the library stayed empty until its original function was forgotten and a new city library was built.

Two or three more examples can speak for the country. In Scituate, Massachusetts, a refugee from medieval France found its way to a hill above the town and took on a new lease of life as the Lawson Water Tower, an Azay-le-Rideau in New England. Thomas Lawson was a financier who cornered the copper market at the end of the nineteenth century. He lived at the bottom of a gentle hill in a house called Dreamwold, and he had to look up at the ugly metal water

ARCHITECTURAL FOLLIES IN AMERICA

tank that supplied water to Scituate. In 1902 it cost Lawson $60,000 to reclothe it as the shingled beauty we see today, and in addition he threw in ten bells to provide a modest carillon for the town. They still strike every quarter hour. The tower was restored in 1976 at a cost of $120,000. Lawson's true folly was the sin of political incorrectness: in 1922 he published a book called *Frenzied Finance*, which revealed how Wall Street manipulated the stock market. Irritated, Wall Street manipulated him and he died penniless two years later. How strange that the tower is roofed in shingles rather than copper.

At the same time in Saint Louis, Missouri, an absurdly tall structure rose on Compton Hill—a square tower of banded brick capped with a cloche hat dome and partnered by an even taller stair turret with an elongated conical roof in the notably rare Disneyland style. There is also a very fine water tower on top of the hill in Eden Park, Cincinnati, Ohio, with a handsome plaque reading "American Water Landmark Significant in the History of Public Water Supply," but we are not told the architect, nor its date.

The Dole Corporation's 10,000-gallon tin pineapple was America's most exotic water tower.

America's most exotic water tower is under serious threat as I write and will have been lost to us before you read this. It was built in 1928 as a 10,000-gallon water tank for the fire control system at the head offices of the Dole Pineapple Corporation in Honolulu, Hawaii, and was designed by Sydney D. Walker in the shape of a pineapple. The Dole Corporation is too busy moving into hotels and the leisure market to concern itself with the fruit that made its fortune, and the prettily painted tin pineapple, 195 feet above the ground, is now surplus to requirements. Its loss will be mourned in years to come.

Utilitarian fire towers were built as observation posts, somewhere to see from rather than to be seen. Prospect towers—located in the most beautiful parts of the country to take advantage of splendid vistas—are just as worthy of attention as the views they serve. In 1922 Bert L. Vaughn of Jacumba, California, was driven to build a monument to the pioneers who opened up the arid southern California desert. He erected a tower in Mountain Springs Pass by the side of

No architect was ever allowed to mar the cheerful innocence of the Vaughn Desert View Tower.

U.S. Route 80, looking east over the Salton Sea and the Imperial Valley towards Seeley and El Centro. It is a crude but robust creation consisting of a rough stone cylinder punctuated by projecting wooden roof beams known as vigas, perched on top of a slightly larger cylinder. Square windows were bought off the shelf and installed at a 45-degree angle to make diamond shapes set randomly in the walls; clearly no architect was allowed near to mar its cheerful innocence. In 1947 the tower, by then abandoned, was bought by Dennis A. Newman who topped off the ensemble with a wooden belvedere roof and the inevitable gift shop around the base. Then the interstate highway came through, and the Desert View Tower returned to its quiet contemplation of the great valley, disturbed by fewer and fewer visitors. A tapering cone of a tower, also called the Desert View Tower, was built by the Fred Harvey Company out of local stone on the edge of the Grand Canyon in 1932, enabling visitors dissatisfied with the eyeball-blistering view of the canyon from 7,500 feet to see it from 7,570 feet. Its semiruinous state is deliberate, to echo the architectural style of the mysterious Anasazi Indians, whose dwellings huddle under the fantastic overhangs of the Canyon de Chelly.

Paterson, New Jersey, does not rank with the Grand Canyon as the epitome of scenic loveliness, but when Catholina Lambert built his castle on a ridge overlooking the town in 1892, it was rather more rural than it is today. The view was such that he added Belle Vista Tower a little further up the hill. Lambert was a short, romantic, hard-headed businessman. Born into poverty in Yorkshire, England, he arrived in America at the age of seventeen with five pounds in his pocket. Within seven years he owned his own silk manufacturing company and had married Belle Shattuck, the daughter of an old Massachusetts family. This was not simply an aggressive man making his way in the world; Lambert was wholly in love. At the foot of the stairs in Lambert Castle was a large, empty, ornate oak picture frame carved with fruit and flowers, placed so that Lina would look up and see Belle Lambert descending the stairs, as pretty as a picture. Belle Vista Tower, gently punning his wife's name, was built in 1896, seventy feet tall with a panoramic vista. It was not an elegant building but like its owner it exuded solidity and dignity. When the state took over Paterson Park the bottom of the tower was used as a snack concession until the late 1960s, but now the concession has been burned out and the tower is severely vandalized. The structure is stout enough to withstand random acts of dilapidation, but it must be seen as being seriously under threat.

Casco Castle in Maine had more obvious attractions. Perched above Freeport with a view over hills and sea, it seemed as good a site as any for a vacation resort. The year 1902 saw the opening of the Casco Castle Hotel, a cheap and cheerful resort destination where vacationers could dine on the hotel's famous Shore Dinner for fifty cents: lobster stew, steamed clams with drawn butter, plain boiled lobster, fried clams, bread and butter, doughnuts, Heinz pickles, cookies, tea, milk, and coffee. The hotel itself was a clapboarded wooden castle, properly arrayed with towers and battlements. Gaily striped awnings were, however, hideously out of character with the mock medieval effect. Soon the need for something more substantial arose, so a round stone prospect tower was built, connected to the hotel by an aerial walkway. The hotel enjoyed great success for several years, but by 1914 business had dropped off and the enterprise was sold. Later that year it caught fire and was burned to the ground. Nothing whatever survives of the wooden castle. Trees have grown up to cover

Castle keepsakes: Left, the sadly derelict Belle Vista Tower no longer lives up to its name; right, this stone prospect tower is all that survives of the once-bustling Casco Castle Hotel.

the bare, rocky ridge along which it stretched, and the land has been divided into separate lots. Only the stone tower survives, an unguessable enigma to those who never knew its history. Peeking out above the trees, surrounded by frame houses, it is a hollow memento of its wooden parent staring blindly out over Casco Bay.

On a tiny peninsula staring out over Otsego Lake in Cooperstown, New York, is an enchanting little 20-foot-square castle with battered walls attached to a 60-foot-tall, 5-story tower. I know it is enchanting because I have seen postcards of it. I have also seen it clearly from the town three miles away, and I have driven right past it, but I have never found it. Searching, I drove into a small estate where a large old man was washing his car. "Hi! How're you doin'?" he greeted me affably. "I wonder if you can help me. I'm looking for Kingfisher Tower," I ventured. Big smile. "You know what?" Big slap on my back. "I'm not gonna help you." Whistling cheerily, he went back to washing his car, leaving me standing puzzled and foolish in his driveway. Welcome to Cooperstown—now go home. The tower (one assumes there are kingfishers on the lake, but they seem as shy as the car washer seemed to be friendly) was built in 1876 by Henry Hardenburgh for Edward Clark, who wanted to relieve unemployment. This is the classic folly story in Europe, where the wildest structures were always excused on the grounds that they relieved unemployment. It was never going to be a long-term solution. Grumpy and embittered, I left, the only man ever to visit Cooperstown without going to the baseball museum.

Anson Phelps Stokes, who made a fortune in mining and railroad development, built the massive Shadowbrook estate in Berkshire, Massachusetts, which was later bought by Andrew Carnegie. The Phelps Stokeses enjoyed their riches and entertained lavishly. Their

Without parties or debutantes to divert him, Anson Phelps Stokes abandoned his Nevada hideaway after only two months.

ARCHITECTURAL FOLLIES IN AMERICA

son J. G. Phelps, at Yale in 1896, telegraphed his mother, "Would like to bring some '96 fellows for the weekend." Mother responded, "Many guests already here. Have only room for fifty." Shadowbrook, although huge, was not a castle, and neither was Stokes Castle, although it has become known as such. Stokes Castle is a small, square three-story tower built by Anson Phelps Stokes not as a weekend retreat but as a true get-away-from-it-all two thousand miles from home. It stands 6,500 feet up in the Shoshone Mountains of Nevada, near Austin, just off the old Pony Express route, sometimes known as the "loneliest road in America." Phelps Stokes forged a railroad through here—Railroad Pass is 6,431 feet high— and built Stokes Tower, as he called it, between 1896 and 1897 as a summer home for his sons. It was built of solid granite and modeled on a medieval tower Stokes had seen near Rome. Lavishly furnished, it was used for two months in the summer of 1897, then abandoned forever. The air is still fresh and clear up in the Shoshones, but there were not many balls and parties to attend, nor debutantes to divert, nor room to entertain fellows. Just the clear clean air, the lovely, lonely views, and the silence, nowadays punctuated by the crack of jets breaking the sound barrier.

If we are serious in our quest for views, then San Francisco is as good a place as any to find them. We must be grateful to Lillie Hitchcock Coit, former fifteen-year-old mascot of the Knickerbocker No. 5 Volunteer Fire Company who, in 1929, left money for the building of a monument to beautify San Francisco. This resulted in an Art Moderne tower on Telegraph Hill, designed by Arthur Brown, Jr., completed in 1934, and popularly thought to commemorate Lillie's husband and the volunteer firemen of the 1850s and 1860s. The tower looks like the nozzle of a fireman's hose. Coincidence, say the historians, who point to a statue down in Washington Square that is the Coit's actual memorial to the city's firefighters. But slightly salacious stories have a way of being more readily remembered. A slow elevator takes you to the glassed-in but open-to-the-sky observation gallery 560 feet above sea level, from where the view is just as fine as you might hope.

Another California belvedere scarcely merits the description of tower, as it is probably just higher than it is wide. It is the sixteen-square-foot Teahouse on Fannette Island, in Emerald Bay on Lake Tahoe, built in 1929 for Mrs. Lora Josephine Knight of Vikingsholm Castle. It is a stark, rough block of a building perched craggily on the famous lake's only island—a tiny tower on a tiny island in a tiny bay on a big lake. Looking like a humpbacked whale in the still clear waters of the bay, the island is the perfect fantasy kingdom for a child, small enough to explore, big enough to defend, and fully equipped with its own ready-made castle tower. It can be visited between June and January, but it is off limits in the spring to allow the nesting birds some solitude.

The Teahouse—a tiny tower perched atop a crag—surveys the fantasy kingdom of Lake Tahoe's Fannette Island.

Ever since Jesuit missionaries first visited China, the pagoda has been a popular style for buildings of leisure in the West. America's pagodas tend to look more to Europe than to the Orient for their models, and the majority of them are to be found along the eastern seaboard rather than the west coast, as might have been expected.

ARCHITECTURAL FOLLIES IN AMERICA

The word *pagoda* is derived from a Portuguese attempt at a Persian word, *but-kadah*, meaning a house of idols. Originally they were towers placed centrally in a temple complex, but quite early on in their development—about the seventh century A.D.—they were removed from their axial role and replaced by great assembly halls, which shared the characteristic upswung eave. American pagodas tend to be squatter than their forebears, and their interpretation has concentrated on the upswung eaves rather than the diminishing stories. Many American pagodas resemble these assembly halls rather than a pagoda tower; one example dating from 1902 actually was built as an assembly hall for a school in Coconut Grove, Miami, by the Buffalo, New York, firm of Greene and Wicks. Despite its name and barely discernible upswinging eaves, the two-story Ransom Everglades School Pagoda looks about as Chinese as a hamburger. Swabbed in a dull green institutional paint job, its only apparent merit is its longevity.

American pagodas do tend to be squatter than their Asian forebears, but the Ransom School Pagoda looks about as Chinese as a hamburger.

The grandest pagoda is to be found high on a hillside overlooking Reading, Pennsylvania. An early morning visit shows it at its best, mysterious and enigmatic in the swirling mist, the town shrouded in the valley below. This is a big, solid building, locked into the hillside by ten tons of bolts, resolutely disdaining the ethereal quality of its Japanese antecedents. It needs the mist to allow it some grace. It was built in 1908 by William Abbot Witman, Sr., at a

Big, solid, and bolted to the hillside, this Reading, Pennsylvania, pagoda needs the morning mist to lend it some grace.

cost of $50,000 as a tea and coffee house, and contemporary photographs show the eaves strung with electric lights making it visible for many miles. Conflicting accounts credit the design to Witman and the construction to William Stout and Howard Jacobs, but a plaque placed on the recently refurbished building remembers James Matz, carpenter, contractor, and builder from his sons Charles E. and James A. Matz, "designers of this pagoda." It was given to the City of Reading in 1911 by Mr. and Mrs. Jonathan Mould, and it is excellently preserved, with the window frames painted dark burgundy and the stonework protected by a polyurethane glaze so that the building gleams and glistens in the early morning dew. Each of the reported seven floors (I could only count six) reduces by two feet in size and the eaves spring up at the ends with a disarming ferocity. Despite the visual intrusion of the brick chimney stack perforating the five tiled roofs and the wholly inappropriate neoclassical molded stone balustrade surrounding the pagoda, this is an impressive and much loved building.

A sharp contrast with this beauty is the Patterson Park Pagoda in Baltimore, Maryland. Designed by Charles H. Latrobe for the city's Park Commission and built in 1891 for $16,730, it now huddles at the top of the park, peeling, empty, and desolate. Windows are broken and boarded up, and the whole structure feels dejected. As a

Though there's nothing intrinsically Chinese about the Patterson Park Pagoda, it somehow manages to convey an oriental feel.

prospect tower it was once gaudily painted in orange and yellow, octagonal with four stories and viewing platforms on each floor. There is nothing intrinsically Chinese about the design apart from the name. The stories do not reduce, and the eaves do not rise, yet somehow it all feels right. The ensemble conveys an oriental feel— perhaps the heavy eaves of the roof and the upcurved struts at the base, unimportant in themselves, trick the eye into accepting Asian antecedents. As recently as 1984, as a gift from the Taiwanese government, two marble statues of Chinese palace lions were placed to guard the entrance to the pagoda, and in a touching little ceremony their eyes were painted red to awaken them. But the red has long since worn away; the lions sleep, and the building remains unguarded. The friends and volunteers of the Butchers Hill Association tried to raise restoration funds for its centenary, but the Paterson Park Pagoda remains sadly derelict.

The Adirondack holiday camps in upstate New York happily borrowed any architectural style that they felt might please their clientele, and a pagoda, more oriental than most, was duly built at the turn of the century at Pine Tree Point on Upper Saint Regis Lake. But the most extraordinary pagoda in the nation is far away from anywhere. Even the Bismarck *Tribune* admits that Pettibone, North Dakota, with its population of ninety-three, isn't exactly a town you have to drive through to get somewhere. In 1980 Henry Luehr, then in his sixties, won a contract to tear down a local grain elevator. With all the spare lumber, he decided to build his own private pagoda. "I had all this damned lumber around here and I wanted to pile it up. So I piled it up." The end result was a fantastic octagonal 8-story tower, over 80 feet high and topped with an onion dome, completely clad in shiny aluminum printing plates. Each floor has an external balcony, and a ladder leads from one level to the next right up to a trap door in the roof that gives sweeping views over, well, over the North Dakota prairie, really. Luehr has decorated the interior of the tower with all the taste and discernment of a magpie—broken phonograph records, discarded toys, rotary dial telephones, old calendars. The pagoda is not the culmination of his activities. On the same site he has recently completed a 26-foot-high bull called Victor Domino VI, built out of cement, lumber, and chicken wire. Luehr is now in his seventies and still building. We say the bull is completed, but Luehr says, "It's not finished. Nothing is ever finished. You only build it to a point." We wait with bated breath to learn of his latest wonders. "I don't plan to quit. I don't even plan on dying."

Another New York State resort, Mohonk Mountain House, boasts a truly magnificent prospect tower in the Shawangunk Mountains. It is four square with angle buttresses and stoutly constructed of rough granite set high on a bluff, commanding spectacular views and appropriately named Sky Top Tower. This resort has been run by the same family of Quakers since 1869, and they are proud of their heritage of conservation. They still have strict rules about alcohol and smoking (no private bottles allowed) but have now relaxed their guest policy, which formerly stipulated (in very small type) "No Hebrews."

Florida boasts a number of towers of varying degrees of utility. One was built to indulge a passion, another to provide a view, a third to test a theory, a fourth to supply water, and a fifth was purely a financial folly. The passion indulged was bell ringing. Edward R. Bok was a Dutch immigrant who made his fortune through magazines, including the *Ladies' Home Journal.* In the heart of Florida at

Edward Bok wrote that his Singing Tower was built "to preach the gospel and influence of beauty."

Mountain Lake, on what he and the national survey thought was the Sunshine State's highest peak—all 324 feet of it—Bok built his Gothic Singing Tower, a mighty belfry of pink and gray marble and coral stone called coquina. Time after time these wonderful structures make us ask *why?*, and all too rarely are we allowed an answer. Edward Bok anticipated the question and wrote: "The purpose of it all? Simply to preach the gospel and influence of beauty reaching out to visitors through tree, shrub, flowers, birds, superb architecture, the music of bells, and the sylvan setting." The tower's architect, Milton B. Medary, claimed that the only specification Bok gave for the tower was that it should be beautiful, but Bok himself wrote that it should be "the most beautiful Carillon Tower in the world . . . a tower as beautiful as that at Malines, Belgium." Bok Tower bears only a passing resemblance to the elaborately buttressed 320-foot Belgian tower, which is still unfinished after nearly 550 years because of religious disagreements and lack of funds.

When Polk County was later resurveyed, Bok's 324-foot mountain was diminished to 295 feet and lost its title of the highest land in Florida to a positively Himalayan 345 feet up in Walton County. Bok may not have been hungering for the rugged Alpine scenery of his native Holland when he chose this mild southern eminence to site his tower, but he was certainly influenced by the strong tradition of carillons in the Low Countries. In the tower he placed one of the largest carillons in the world, 57 bronze bells imported from Loughborough, England, weighing from 17 pounds to 12 tons. Medary determined the size and shape of the tower after consulting carillon experts and a representative from the bell founders, John Taylor and Company. He was told that the bellchamber needed to be 35 feet wide and 50 feet high, and the lowest bell should be at least 150 feet from the ground. The finished tower, at 205 feet, really is a masterpiece. The materials used are exquisite both to look at and in name, the salmon-pink coral rock called coquina, Georgia marble, gray Creole, and shell-pink Etowah. It is so beautifully constructed that we must applaud the builders, Horace H. Burrell and Son, the stone masons under the direction of master mason Vincent de Benedetto, and Richard Henle, the field director. Visitors are not allowed on the little island on which the tower stands, which is a pity, because the craftsmanship of those workers has to be touched to be believed. President Coolidge came to dedicate the tower and gardens, rich with the song of nightingales that Bok had had imported from England, in January 1929. Less than a year later Bok was dead, happy to have fulfilled his mother's dictum to "make your world a bit better or more beautiful because you have lived in it." The tower, with its attendant mature gardens, is now a thriving commercial venture, like much of Florida. Entry to the gardens is free, but you have to pay to park.

The Singing Tower, built as a carillon, was never designed for public access or as a prospect tower, and the magnificent views to be had from the top (it is higher than a twenty-story building) can only be enjoyed by the garden staff. The views are glimpsed rather than being laid out in a panorama as at the Florida Citrus Tower. This was built in Clermont as a prospect tower, as plain and utilitarian as the Bok Tower is ornate and fanciful, a tower to look from rather than at. It is stark, angular, and white, relieved only by a green and red stripe running the whole 226-foot height of the building. It was the brainchild of A. W. Thacker and F. J. Toole from Pittsburgh, who described it without a trace of humor or self-consciousness as being like a gigantic map-tack. Architecturally it is about as significant as

Described by its builder as a "gigantic map-tack," the Florida Citrus Tower has only its height to commend it.

a map-tack, too, with nothing but its size to commend it. This is presumably why no architect is credited. Thacker and Toole managed to inveigle 240 investors to participate in this monument to the Florida citrus industry, and it is now under its third ownership since it opened in July 1956. Seeing that Florida's two major industries were tourism and citrus, it made sense to combine the two and provide yet another successful attraction to distract visitors from the coagulating climate. And yes, it has a carillon, too.

Less successful was the theory mooted by Richter C. Perky, who reasoned that because bats liked belfries, if he built one the bats would move in, feast on the abundant mosquito life, and instantly free Lower Sugarloaf Key of the pestilential anopheles. Bats would never be allowed to sully the pristine beauty of a belfry like Bok Tower, but things were more free and easy out in the Florida Keys. Up went the Perky Bat Tower, a bizarre wooden structure built for utility rather than beauty, and sure enough, within a few years the Keys were virtually mosquito free. The tower, faintly reminiscent of a cross between a grain hopper and an Egyptian pylon, stands on

DDT—not the Perky Bat Tower—was what finally got rid of Sugarloaf Key's anopheles mosquitoes.

four legs, protected from crawling bugs by metal shields placed around its knees. Inside is an immensely complicated system of shutters, grids, and roosting frames, all beautifully crafted and carpentered. Apparently it was filled with a patented substance sold by a doctor in Houston, Texas, which was supposed to be infallibly attractive to bats but which appears to have been dried bat excrement. It didn't work. DDT rather than Perky's theory did in the mosquitoes. Today Perky's silver-bleached shingled Bat Tower stands lonely, isolated, and bat-free in a little tarmac circle near the Sugarloaf Airfield in the baking Florida Keys. And the bugs are back.

Clearly seen from Interstate 275 is a round white tower like a castellated pencil on the banks of the Hillsborough River in Tampa, Florida. It is said to be an ordinary water tower, but has quite clearly been "improved" to provide a viewing platform at the top in its two-

Utterly plain but for its garnish of battlements, this Tampa water tower is nevertheless immensely attractive.

ARCHITECTURAL FOLLIES IN AMERICA

story belvedere, which is ringed with battlements. There is something immensely attractive about this simple white water tower, utterly plain except for its little garnish of mock medieval defenses.

One attempted definition of a folly, far from all-embracing, is that it is a building that has swallowed up a great deal of money for little return. On that count one of the biggest follies in the nation is the CenTrust Tower, an opulent office building in Miami constructed by disgraced savings and loan banker David L. Paul. It cost $175 million to build, some $13.2 million of which went to pay for a painting by Rubens in Paul's home. Paul's Folly was sold by federal regulators in June 1991 for $44 million. Who took the $131 million loss on the tower? That's right—the American taxpayer. Another attempted definition of folly goes like this: orthodoxy rules that form follows function, therefore, when a building patently fails to adhere to that form or fulfill that function or, even worse, deliberately sets out to pass itself off as something else, then it must be a folly. Such is the case with two small lighthouses in New York State, one about thirty feet tall tacked onto the side of Taylor's Gas Station in Cooperstown, a good mile away from Lake Otsego, and another stubby little one providing a nautical touch but barely clearing the roof of a bungalow on Island Channel Road in Seaford, Long Island. Both were built in the 1930s, purely from whimsy. Some towers become follies through their mystery, built for a perfectly feasible

Landlubbers: Above, this squat little lighthouse barely clears the roof of the Long Island bungalow to which it's attached; left, the Taylor's Gas Station lighthouse is a mile away from the nearest large body of water.

purpose now forgotten by all but the long forgotten builder. The octagonal four-story tower on Atkinson Common in Newburyport, Massachusetts, was described as "newly built" in 1937 but looks much older. The common was laid out in 1873, and the tower could well predate this. The heavily barred, unglazed windows, increasing in size with the height of the tower, give it a grim, quasi-industrial aspect which prompted a resident to speculate that it must have been built as a jail.

No one knows who built this little tower in Newburyport, Massachusetts, or what on earth its purpose may have been.

ARCHITECTURAL FOLLIES IN AMERICA

There are towers of welcome, towers of pride, towers of victory, towers of memory. For years Honolulu's Eiffel Tower, its Statue of Liberty, its most visible symbol was the Aloha Tower, the welcome tower on the seafront, the tallest building on the islands. It was built by Arthur Reynolds in 1921, a 10-story, 184-foot tower with four clock faces, "Aloha" prominently pasted above each of them, and affording panoramic views. But now it looks slightly swamped by the development all around. In 1993 a man with a fire extinguisher, who said he had a mission from God, smashed the glass of all the clock faces from the inside. What harm had the building done him?

Pride is a great stimulus for building, as we see throughout this book. What motive other than pride prompted Oral Roberts to erect his gilded Prayer Tower in front of his university in Tulsa, Oklahoma? And put yourself in the shoes of the man who builds the tallest building in town, and advertises it as such, only to find that across the street an even taller building is going up, and that if you don't act pretty quickly people might laugh at you. What do you do? You add height. And when it happens again, you add more height. And again, and again. This is the sad story of the pride of Daniel Powers, who completed an office building in downtown Rochester, New York, in 1869, only to find his glory continually sniped at. His big brownstone office building had to acquire a mansard roof to stave off the competition. Then another one, above. Then a roof extension was added. Finally came a tower, raised five stories above the heightened roof line in a last desperate attempt to stay above the Wilder building across the street until Powers's death finally ended the competition. The Powers Building has recently been thoroughly restored to its mid-Victorian glory of brass, marble, and wood.

Commemorating the dead through the building of a tower is a custom as ancient as civilization, one which has lasted thousands of years right up to the twentieth century. On Mount Greylock in Massachusetts a beautiful, smooth tower of Quincy granite, like a land-locked lighthouse, stands 105 feet high, commemorating the soldiers and sailors of the state, while in Winsted, Connecticut, the same function is fulfilled by the Winchester Soldiers' Monument. This is a Civil War monument, built twenty-five years after the fighting finished, at a cost of $13,000. It was designed in the Gothic Revival style by Robert W. Hill after years of argument in the city as to what form the monument should take. What we see is a square castellated three-story tower, only 44 feet high, gently battered at the base, but what really catches the eye is the prominent bartizan tur-

ret topped by the 8-foot, 3-inch statue of a color bearer. The Winchester Soldiers' Monument is special; the dry bones of history hide passions scarlet in their intensity. It took fifteen years to raise $2,500 towards the cost of the monument, but when William L. Gilbert, the town's largest employer, offered $4,000 to the fund in 1887, his offer was unaccountably rejected. Thereafter the cash flowed in, the hilltop land was donated, and the tower was completed within three years. After its erection and dedication the fighting started anew; there was a faction that vehemently disagreed with it, and eventually they put up their own Civil War monument at the other end of town—a conventional statue of a rifleman on a pedestal, donated by Charles H. Pine in 1904.

Only Daniel Powers' death could end his quest to have the tallest building in Rochester, New York.

There is so much more to discover. Driving along the freeway near Meriden, Connecticut, we noticed a castellated round tower on a bluff high above the road. No camera, no books, no maps—the usual well-prepared outing—so we turned off the highway to track the tower down. Just keep turning right and we'll be bound to reach it, I thought. It seemed that every road we turned down had a large black labrador at the end of it, staring inquisitively at us. Two hours later we called it a day. America does not reveal her secrets so easily. Much later we found the facts: the tower can be reached, and it is the centerpiece of Hubbard Park, given to the City of Meriden by Walter Hubbard. Hubbard had traveled the world and had been particularly struck by the scenery at Craigellachie in Scotland, in the good whisky valley of Strathspey. There is indeed a passing similarity to the Hanging Hills of Connecticut, except that the Constitution State is poorly served in the matter of ruined castles. Hubbard set out to remedy the deficit by employing a young Scots draftsman, Stuart Douglass, to design him a castle tower on the summit of East Peak. This dramatic site allows the short rough stone tower to be seen for miles. Castle Craig's dedication ceremony, in October 1900, was marked by an oyster and clam bake, with six barrels of oysters and a barrel of clams being provided by the benevolent Hubbard.

All buildings can stir human emotions. They can be sad, glad, and stranger than we know; they baffle, amuse, cause reverence or awe; they provoke anger or disgust; but in the final analysis towers, like children, simply demand attention. A guest house at the Villa Zapû winery in California's Napa Valley takes the form of a plain, square, unadorned five-story white tower, but its location among the sweeping hills of Saint Helena, its position on a low mound above a swimming pool designed in the tradition of a reflecting pool to echo the tower's form, and the elongated banners flying wildly from the flagpoles extended horizontally from both sides of the tower grant it an ethereal, other-worldly quality rarely found in a modern building. It was built in 1987 by David Connor of the British architects Powell-Tuck Connor and Orefelt. This totally practical building, the antithesis of folly, takes its inspiration from the solitary cry of a folly tower alone in an alien landscape, the building that stands by itself.

The finest pure folly in the United States of America is a group officially known as the Watts Towers of Simon Rodia, standing in a part of Los Angeles better known for anarchy than architecture. Arriving in L.A. for the first time in the summer of 1979, with black storm clouds looming overhead, I asked at the car rental desk for the best way to Watts. The lady laughed. "There is no best way," she said.

An archway from Simon Rodia's Watts Towers: a confection of cans, bottles, tiles, glass, sea shells, and whatever else he could get his hands on.

Then she saw I was serious. "You really don't want to go there. Do you?" I insisted. She recommended extra insurance. So before checking into my hotel, before washing, before shaving, before doing anything, off I went to Watts—the first thing I had to see in California was this extraordinary folly built by an Italian immigrant. It did not disappoint. Indeed it was better than I had hoped for, a cross between the Palais Idéal of the Postman Cheval in France, the Barwick Park Cone in England, and Gaudí's unfinished Sagrada Familia Cathedral in Spain. It is a natural masterpiece.

Simon Rodia was born Sabatino Rodia in Serino, in the province of Avellino, near Naples, Italy, in 1879. He came to America in 1891, to Pennsylvania at first, and worked as a handyman and tile setter. He bought a triangular lot in Los Angeles at the side of a railroad track on East 107th Street in 1921, and two years later he started to build his towers in the back yard—single-handedly, because most of the time he didn't know what he was going to do himself. "I had in mind to do something big, and I did. You have to be *good good* or *bad bad* to be remembered," he is quoted as saying. Over a period of thirty-three years the three main towers—technically they are spires, two linked by apparently fragile arches like cobweb buttresses enclosing hearts—rose up nearly 100 feet from the small triangular lot in a confection of Canada Dry cans, broken tiles, glass, concrete, railroad ties, sea shells, rich blue Milk of Magnesia and green 7-Up bottles, chicken wire, cement, steel rods, and anything else Rodia could lay his hands on. The first spire he completed, the East Tower, is 55 feet high. The second is 97 feet, 10 inches, and the West Tower, his final tall tower, is 99 feet, 6 inches. He built the structures by splicing them with steel mesh and cement mortar—there are no rivets, bolts, or welds anywhere. Nor did he use scaffolding; he climbed the spires as he built them, tying himself on with a window cleaner's belt. Just by the walls of his house is the Cupola, probably intended as an open air meeting place for his evangelical church. He built a fountain in the center, but the city would not allow permission for a water supply.

Comparisons have been drawn between Rodia's towers and the huge portable spires displayed in some Italian towns during religious celebrations, fanciful recreations of medieval spires with ziggurat-style steps spiraling up to the pinnacle. One such is the Macchina di Santa Rosa of Viterbo, brought out on the evening of September 3 each year. This imposing structure—*l'imponente mole*—stands 115 feet high and is brilliantly lit at night. It is an

ARCHITECTURAL FOLLIES IN AMERICA

unforgettable spectacle. An equivalent festival takes place in Nola, forty miles from Rodia's birthplace at Serino. Seen only once a year, it is easy to imagine how such a rare vision could affect an impressionable young boy. Rodia's other strong impression must have been the ship in which he sailed to America. The apex or bow of his triangular lot was called the Ship of Marco Polo, with a 28-foot mast and tile-set hull. What sets Rodia's folly apart from every other such structure (for it is not unique, as you will see in this book) is the sheer elegance of his untutored design and the astonishing use of color throughout. Every part of the entire erection is decorated somehow; either with impressed patterns from simple tools to complex flower molds, or with colored tiles and glass apparently set at random but combining to produce an electrifying effect. The structure continually changes color in the constant California climate. At dawn it is a totally different building than the one seen at dusk. It may not be unique, but it surpasses all others for quality.

At the age of seventy-five in 1954, Sam, as he was known to everyone, stopped building, gave the house, garden, and towers to his neighbor and walked out. His house was burned by vandals the following year, and the Department of Building and Safety ordered the towers to be demolished. They took jackhammers to the structures, failed to make an impression, and retired defeated. The 1933 Long Beach earthquake cracked the foundations of City Hall but had left the towers unscathed. The towers were rescued by William Cartright and Nicholas King, who bought them in 1959 and handed them into the care of the Committee for Simon Rodia's Towers in Watts. Rodia, living with his family in Martinez, near San Francisco, washed his hands of the whole affair. He simply did not want to know—the ultimate "been there, done that" attitude. Now the towers are owned by the State of California and looked after by the Los Angeles Cultural Affairs Department. Now for the *good good* news and the *bad bad* news. Nothing bad happened to me in Watts. The good thing was that in 1979, apart from the rain clouds, I had the site to myself. A little menace, whether human or meteorological, does wonders in lessening congestion. I went back for another visit on a warm Saturday afternoon in 1994. Watts is proud of its towers. They are now safely protected by a stout steel fence, and at least a dozen people were braving the area's rough reputation to pay homage to a masterpiece.

Chapter 2

PAVILIONS OF SPLENDOR

Words change their meanings over the years, and in today's caring and sensitive society meanings change more quickly than ever. What was acceptable ten years ago is today's slur. The word *folly* is a notable exception to the rule. The word began as an epithet of contempt, and it is the shadow of that contempt that adds excitement to their study. Now the title is desirable; it confers a cachet on the building thus honored. Formerly the harmless house with but one feature that distinguished it from its neighbor was immediately castigated as folly. It was an architecturally incorrect statement, which is why we have a rash of buildings labeled So-and-So's Folly. The folly hunter dashes hopefully from state to state ending up with a succession of imposing but otherwise conventional mansions. A list of these appear in the gazetteer at the end of the book; where they are not mentioned in the text you can be sure that the term folly applies to little more than the name. Illustrating this point is the large seminary of Saint Joseph Cupertino, situated off Folly Quarter Road in the sleek rolling farmland of northern Maryland. The seminary building, a gracious

When Charles Carroll heard his son was planning to build this small mansion, he snorted "Folly!"

but hefty gray stone house once called Folly Quarter Mansion, was built in 1832 by Charles Carroll of Carrolton's son. When he heard his son was planning to build a small mansion, Carroll, the only signatory of the Declaration of Independence uncertain enough to need to append his hometown, snorted "Folly!" That is the whole story. Folly Castle in Petersburg, Virginia, is neither a folly nor a castle—it was built in 1763 by Peter Jones II and called Folly Castle by the locals because they felt it was too large for a childless man. Jones was merely planning ahead; he went on to sire a house full.

Gothic architecture and follies are inseparable, but there are several Greek Revival houses that have appropriated the name. The 1852 Pitt's Folly in Uniontown, Alabama, has mighty Doric colonnades on only two sides, which may be the reason for its name, while there seems even less reason for the naming of Manning's Folly, a heptastyle mansion in Pinewood, South Carolina. There is Joseph Smith's Folly in Staunton, Virginia, built in 1818; Morris's Folly in Whitemarsh, Pennsylvania, built by Samuel Morris in 1750 for his young bride who left him before it was finished; and the list goes on. None of these offers an explanation for its name. Maris's Folly in New Hope, Pennsylvania, on the New Jersey line, is an

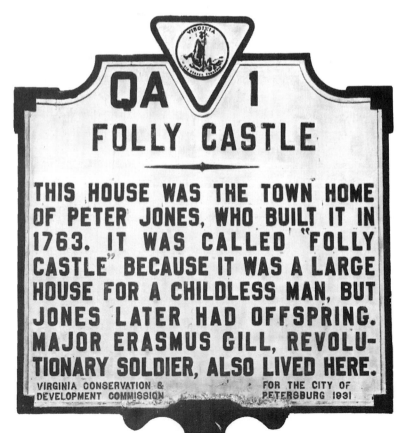

What's in a name? Folly Castle, in Petersburg, Virginia, was neither folly nor castle.

artist's colony. The use of *folly* seems to be random: Jessie Pearson converted a bridge across the Blackwater River in Virginia into a house, which immediately became Pearson's Folly, while up in New York a covered bridge built in 1920 to carry the state road over Black Creek in Bundyville was converted into a house a few years later by Edward Corpron, when the road was rerouted. The Woodside family acquired and extended the property in 1936, and it is now known as the Woodside House rather than Woodside's Folly.

There is a grand house on Main Street in Newburyport, Massachusetts, Dexter's Folly, which has no trace of folly about it. It was originally built for Jonathan Jackson in 1771, but its second owner added eccentricity by the bucket load. Timothy Dexter was so eccentric he would have been locked away as mad had he not been so rich. Tales abound of his bizarre behavior. He staged his own funeral,

Perhaps Timothy Dexter's greatest folly was not his grand house, but his eccentric lifestyle.

then beat his wife for not grieving sufficiently. So irritated was he by her lack of grief that he commissioned a poet to write her epitaph, and thenceforth referred to her as "the gost." Eventually he gave her $2,000 to leave him, and advertised for a new wife. After a thirteen-year wait during which not one application was received, he sent his "gost" money to come back to him—which she did. Dexter's money came from intuitive fortune; he was a poor tanner who collected worthless scrip issues that suddenly became valid when Alexander Hamilton and Thomas Jefferson set up the national bank, making him the richest man in town. With his new capital he embarked on a series of deranged speculations: he sold coals to Newcastle (the English were on strike), cats to a mouse-ridden island, warming pans to the West Indies (for dipping molasses), and cleared a fortune with each transaction. Dexter's immortality is assured by a book he published in 1801 entitled *A Pickle For The Knowing Ones.* A brief extract will show why:

> Ime the first Lord in the younited States of Amercary Now of Newburyport it is the voise of the people and I cant Help it and so Let it goue Now as I must be Lord there will foller many more Lords pretty soune for it dont hurt A Cat Nor the mouse Nor the son Nor the water Nor the Eare then goue on all is Easey Now bons broaken all is well all in love Now I begin to Lay the corner ston and the kee ston with grat Remembrance of my father Jorge Washington the grate herow

Percipient readers may have noticed a scarcity of regular punctuation, but Dexter had prepared for those carping eyes. Two pages at the end of the book consisted of nothing but punctuation marks, with instructions to "solt and peper" the text to taste. Perhaps Dexter's folly was his lifestyle.

When you design and build your own house you are unfettered by the unimaginative concepts of others. A good architect can assess your needs with meticulous care and produce an eminently practical building to your budget. A great architect will impose his devices and desires upon you—often the client is a stepping stone to his greatness. But people's wants and needs change, growing and diminishing while the architecture remains static. In general, people have to adapt to their houses rather than the other way round. This is not acceptable to some people; it certainly was not good enough for Jule Körner, an artist in Kernersville, North Carolina. He set out, in 1880, to build himself a compact and convenient house with a studio and stables. But, to a farmer passing by, the layout must have seemed extravagant as he said, "That will surely be Jule Körner's folly." Körner liked the name, and the house has been known since its inception as Körner's Folly. After its modest beginnings, Körner's house was continually adapted to his constantly changing requirements, which seem to have been neverending once he married. It ended up with twenty-two rooms on seven levels, some with 25-foot ceilings and others with 6-foot ceilings. Eight sizes of handmade brick were used. Körner's Folly also contains built-in furniture of such a size that it cannot be moved, a theater, and a completely fireproof room where visitors were permitted to smoke. From the outside the most notable feature of the house is the extraordinary narrowness of the windows: they punch through the walls like exclamation marks. Could it be that the name inspired the eccentricity?

> I keep six honest serving-men
> (They taught me all I knew).
> Their names are What and Why and When,
> And How and Where and Who.

The most inquisitive and most elusive of Kipling's honest serving-men is *Why*. In a hamlet between Kennebunk and Kennebunkport, Maine, stands a pinnacled and crocketed Gothic fantasy known as the Wedding Cake House. We know what the house is, where it is, who built it, how and when it was done, but there is nothing in the life of George W. Bourne, industrious and respected shipwright of The Landing, Kennebunk, to account for why this sudden eruption of glorious Gothic decoration frosted the exterior of a comfortable but previously unexceptional family home. This is such a house as dreams are made of, but we know nothing of Bourne's dream. He was driven by the same urge we see throughout this book. A man retires and instead of getting itchy feet, he gets itchy hands. Once the building bug has bitten, the disease cannot be eradicated. It seems to have begun innocently enough when, in 1852, Bourne needed to rebuild his barn and shed connecting them to his house, which had burned down the previous winter. This project coincided with his retirement from his shipyard. Now he had time on his hands, and he utilized it by decorating his new barn and the connecting wall in picture-book Gothic with arches, buttresses, pinnacles and gables, making an eye-catcher of impressive size. The work took about two years, and at the same time Bourne added a latticed Gothic canopy porch to the front of the

To create his Wedding Cake House, George Bourne added fanciful Gothic ornamentation to an otherwise ordinary structure.

house. Then in 1855, Julia Ann Kingsbury, the daughter of Bourne's shipbuilding partner Henry, wrote "Uncle George is fixing the carved work on his house to match the barn." What a mild announcement for such a spectacular accomplishment! It took two summers to cage the old house in its Gothic finery, created in Bourne's imagination and executed by him and Thomas Durrell, a young apprentice who was staying at the house. Angled corner buttresses, Tudor arched spandrels of lacelike fretwork, tiny castellations, an exquisite confection. It was completed in the summer of 1856, and Bourne, his life's work at an end, died that December. A clue to his inspiration was provided by his grandson George Bourne Lord in 1929: "Grandfather Bourne was a great case to draw. After his death we found many drawings he had made of the Cathedral at Milan," and indeed the crocketed pinnacles so typical of that extraordinary structure are faithfully echoed in this southern Maine village.

Despite preconceptions that Switzerland is a nation of cuckoo-clock carvers living in chalets with huge eaves and balconies draped with geraniums, the average Swiss in reality is more likely to be a banker living in a high-rise apartment. If you really want to see Swiss chalets, it is easier to take a trip to the Cincinnati area, where you will find Swiss chalets in the suburb of Hyde Park, four of them alone in one block on Reading Road. Cincinnati was heavily settled by Germans, and the gemütlich architecture of Bavaria and Switzerland was a powerful reminder of home. In the Walnut Hills district you will discover not only the finest Swiss chalet in America but one that is the equal of any in Switzerland. This really was a labor of love. Albert D. Fischer, a nineteenth-century industrialist who immigrated from Hanover, Germany, made his money in preserving and bottling, and in 1890 he commissioned the architect Lucien F. Plympton of Nash and Plympton to build his dream house, inspired by the prototypical Alpine dwelling. It was not simply a copy. The exterior oiled and stained cypress wood and the load-bearing wooden beams were crafted in Switzerland, and many of the decorations were also imported. From the back of the house—three stories at the front, five at the back—there used to be extensive views of the Ohio River,

The Fischer chalet, in Cincinnati, Ohio, is the equal of any found in Switzerland.

ARCHITECTURAL FOLLIES IN AMERICA

but tree growth and tower block development have obliterated the views. Such an extraordinary sight in a smart residential district prompted some adverse comment at the time of building. Gazing on the thirty colors in which the chalet was painted, the contemporary Cincinnati magazine *Chic* dubiously reassured readers that "time and the effects of weather will better prove the architect's theory" and, moreover, that "Swiss architecture is of Grecian origin and has little or nothing to do with surrounding styles." The present owner combats the effects of weather by having the house entirely repainted every five years. It takes 310 hours, and it looks wonderful. Cincinnati is not the only Little Switzerland in America; the town of Helen, Georgia, is remarkable for its Alpine façades and there is a replica of a Swiss village in New Glarus, Wisconsin.

The Carson House of Eureka, California, is considered the empress of the "painted ladies."

The "Painted Ladies," as they are affectionately known, are the West Coast manifestations of the mysteriously named Queen Anne style of architecture—late Victorian polychromatic flamboyance, joyfully thieving elements from the preceding eighty years with eclectic abandon. There are marvelous examples of such Victoriana to be found all over America, from Cape May, New Jersey, to San Francisco, but the apogee of the style, the empress of them all, is the Carson House in Eureka, California. This is an explosion of carpentry, a fountain of gables, turrets, windows, and balconies, a veritable wooden wonder, where the only restraint shown is in the rather drab color scheme, a dull olive green and buff. William Carson was a lumber baron who is said to have built the mansion during a slump in the lumber industry, to relieve unemployment. More than one hundred carpenters worked on the house for two years beginning in 1884, and when it was completed Carson went on to use the same architects, Samuel and Joseph Newcombe of San Francisco, to build a pretty little pink palace across the street as a wedding present for his son. The Carson House stands prominently at the top of Second Street, dominating the downtown, as assertive a piece of architecture as you will ever see. It is said to be the most photographed Victorian house in America. In excellent condition, it now houses the Ingomar Club, a private organization dedicated to its preservation.

The silver miner E. J. "Lucky" Baldwin's estate, also in California, is at the heart of the Los Angeles State and County Arboretum in Arcadia. The arboretum was originally Baldwin's ranch, and his cheery little cherry-red and white guest house was a slender, fragile, three-story octagonal tower that has survived 125 years of earthquakes, floods, and fires. Where the Carson mansion impresses

This little pink
palace stands
across from the
Carson House.

through size and bombast, Lucky Baldwin's gingerbread cottage and tower, designed by A.A. Bennett, charms through scale and setting.

Inevitably we will come across the word *folly* where no folly can be found. The term has been applied to brooks and streams in Connecticut; Folly Brooks in Hartford and Wethersfield were probably named in the mid-seventeenth century, long before the word generally came to be applied to buildings. This may have derived from Norman French: a copse of trees was often described as *feuillée*, "leaved," and the word migrated into vernacular English as folly. It is quite possible that a shady, overhung brook could have been described as Folly Brook by an immigrant from Hampshire or Berkshire.

In eighteenth-century Maryland it seemed to be the natural description of someone else's house, whether through jealousy, spite, or jest we cannot tell, but we now have misleading names such as Connick's Folly in Baden, Folly Farm in Fairhaven, and Clocker's Fancy in Saint Mary's City; venerable but otherwise unremarkable houses, not a folly among them. Annapolis holds the folly tradition for the state with a splendid story of simmering intrigue that began when Thomas Bladen, American born but English educated, was appointed governor of Maryland colony in 1742. His first act was to build himself a vast mansion to reflect his status, but before he could finish it he was ejected and sent back to England. He had been authorized by the assembly to buy four acres of land to build "a Dwelling-house and other Conveniences for the Residence of the Governor of Maryland for the time being, the cost not to exceed £4,000." Two years later he went back to the assembly to seek a further £2,000 to finish the work, but the assembly had had enough. In 1762 Benjamin Mifflin from Philadelphia visited Annapolis:

Left unfinished by the colonial governor who began it, Bladen's Folly was eventually topped off with a cupola.

"Viewed Bladens Folly as the Inhabitants Call it, the ruins of a Spacious Building began by Govr Bladen but carried no further than the Brick Work & Joists 2 stories High but if finished would have been a Beautifull Edifice." For nearly forty years Bladen's Folly stood empty and unfinished, until pragmatism arrived with the Revolution. The building was completed with an octagonal drum and monopteros cupola on the roof, and it stands today as McDowell Hall, Saint John's College, having been reconstructed in 1909 after a devastating fire. Mifflin's description of a building as a folly in this context is the earliest direct use of the word in the English language, predating any similar usage in Britain.

The Spadina House's screaming gables can really frighten children, even in the Beverly Hills sunshine.

In Reserve, Louisiana, a splendid Steamboat Gothic house was built by Valsin Marmillion in 1849. It is called San Francisco, but that is a corruption of its original name. Marmillion spared nothing to build the grandest house he could afford. It turned out to be grander than he could afford; it cost him everything he had, even before work started on the 70-by-60-foot ballroom. At least he retained a sense of humor in his penury, naming the house *Saint-Frusquin*—French slang for "the whole kit and caboodle"—which was bastardized into San Francisco.

Pavilions of splendor are created both by the independently wealthy, who can afford to disregard convention, and the independently poor, who may not have money to spare but are also unaffected by the opinions of others. Problems arise when the desire for an individual creation runs counter to the accepted, expected pattern of building. David A. Campbell was professor of architectural engineering at Penn State in the 1920s. Campbell tried to create a personal house without the simple disregard for custom or regulations shown by the scrap shack builders or the wealth and influence of the rich. He knew what he wanted to build: an amalgam of Arthurian legend and the Arts and Crafts movement. Raising the capital to fund it, however, was predictably problematic. The contractor even made Campbell promise not to reveal his identity in case he was laughed at. The result, after fifteen years in the building, was Camelot, apparently inspired by the wayside inns of England. The house is stuccoed, with rough fieldstone surrounds to the windows and door. Its asymmetric styling, sweeping roof lines, panoply of gables, and deep eaves create a hodgepodge of rustic and European vernacular, a good example of proto-Disney architecture.

California must have the most extraordinary individual piece of domestic architecture in America—the Spadina House in Beverly

Hills, on the corner of Carmelita and Walden. We have all been conditioned to know what a witch's house looks like, and here it is. With high, screaming gables; a tumble-down, rolling roof, not thatched as everyone expects but randomly roofed with cedar shingles; tiny windows that cry out for a pointed hat to glare through; and bizarre asymmetrical shutters, this is one building that can really frighten children even in the sunshine. With its 90210 zip code, it is set in the middle of one of the most desirable slices of real estate in the nation. A closer inspection after the initial visual shock shows that this is a well cared for and well loved home.

Conrad Schuck was a building contractor from Pittsburgh who was given one year to live by his doctors. He relocated to Bartow, Florida, where, in 1924, he began to build his dream house. Excavating the foundations, Schuck found a solid rock bed, so he used the stone to build the house. Apart from the odd train rail used for reinforcement and the imported tiles for decoration, the whole house was created from the materials on site. Ingenious touches abound: before air conditioning was generally available the house was built in a cruciform design with a central fireplace, allowing for through breezes on hot summer days. The columns of the porches were hollow to catch rainwater, which provided additional cooling. The living room had removable ceiling panels, so each one could be taken down and decorated with ease. A huge lazy Susan in the kitchen not only served as that room's entire cabinet system but also revolved around the column containing the house's electrical circuitry, all of which still works today. Schuck's one year to live became forty, and when he finally died the house was bought by Lucy DuCharme, who has lived there for thirty years. Seventy years on, the Wonder House still works, thanks no doubt to Shuck's Germanic thoroughness and DuCharme's loving maintenance. Only the fireplace no longer functions, because during the Second World War Shuck was accused of using a system of mirrors to signal messages up the chimney to German airplanes overhead. Not many German airplanes violated Florida airspace during the war, and anyway Schuck was Austrian, but nevertheless he stoically filled in the chimney with concrete. Whose was the folly?

"It's got a kind of tacky charm about it that's hard to define," said friends in Chicago about the House of the Rock south of Spring Green, Wisconsin. And they were right, if you happen to believe that a house with an 80-foot-diameter carousel, and a room 218 feet long overhanging a valley 150 feet below and which started off by being accessible only by rope ladder could be tacky. It started in the 1940s,

when artist Alex Jordan found the ideal site for a hermitage on a 60-foot limestone chimney outcrop on a hillside near Frank Lloyd Wright's hometown. He built a single-roomed studio on the top of the chimney, hauling materials up with a pulley, and over the years he added to it in an organic sort of way that Wright would have approved of, each accretion fitting into the natural shape of the rock, building around trees so that they grew inside and outside the house. People began to hear about the studio and wanted to come visit. Jordan would throw down his rope ladder, they would clamber up, admire, and clamber down again. Being nobody's fool, Jordan figured that they might also pay if asked, so he did. Fifty years later the quiet little get-away-from-it-all hermitage attracts well over a half million visitors a year and has grown to include twenty buildings spread over 530 acres. This involuntary theme park has allowed Jordan to indulge in some bizarre exploits, offering for the delight of visitors a huge collection of nickelodeons and fairground instruments as well as the World's Largest Crystal Chandelier, the World's Largest Fireplace, the World's Largest Steam Tractor, the World's Largest Carousel, the World's Largest Theater Organ, and the World's Largest Perpetual Motion Clock. The crash of cymbals and calliope, of orchestrion and organ whistle through the once peaceful valley. Tacky, perhaps; self-indulgent, maybe; but profitable? Certainly.

Conrad Schuck's Wonder House, built entirely from materials found on site, still works today.

Boathouses are garages for boats; houseboats are boats for living in. It is unusual but not eccentric to live in a boat, unless the boat is made of plaster and plywood and built solidly on dry land. S.S. *Encinitas 732* and S.S. *Moonlight 726* are neither boathouses nor houseboats; they are houses built in the shape of boats, moored on Third Street between F and G in Encinitas, California, with the blue Pacific beating on the beach behind the hill like a bad child, heard but not seen. The closest they come to water is when it rains. They were built as homes in 1929 by Miles Kellogg, a retired marine engineer, allegedly from materials salvaged from the demolition of the Moonlight Beach Dance Pavilion and the Encinitas Hotel. A surfer rents S.S. *Encinitas*, and has lived there for three years. "I guess my friends think it's pretty cool," he remarks modestly.

Neither houseboat nor boathouse, the S.S. *Encinitas* gets wet only when it rains.

ARCHITECTURAL FOLLIES IN AMERICA

Real houseboats can be found in every shape and size at Waldo Point in Sausalito, over the Golden Gate Bridge in Marin County. The only requirement for such a structure is that it floats; it need do nothing so inconvenient as move through the water, so there is no need for prows or bows or any such nautical appendages. The boat people have taken full advantage of this architectural freedom and devised a number of wild and woolly layouts, ranging from floating trailer homes to a cedar shingle interpretation of Jørn Utzon's Sydney Opera House. The fundamental difference between the Taj Mahal in India and the Taj Mahal in Sausalito is that the California version floats. There are other substantial differences of course, but the first impression given by this waterside wonder in San Francisco Bay is distinctly Moorish. Sausalito's Taj shuns the company of lesser

The boathouses at Waldo Point in Sausalito are floating fantasies.

This Sausalito-style Taj Mahal doesn't just float—it also has an elevator and a Jacuzzi.

boathouses and instead floats in splendor at the end of a pier in the marina, deep in a leafless forest of masts. It started life in the 1960s as a design by architects Charles Porter and Robert Steindewell for a single floating room moored in the bay. The second owner decided to make some alterations. It now has three stories, an elevator, two kitchens (one gas, one electric), marble fireplaces, four bedrooms, three bathrooms, a Jacuzzi (this *is* California), and a passing resemblance to every Moorish building ever seen. The Taj Mahal is, of course, Mogul not Moorish, but this version is undeniably impressive.

When a downtown apartment block starts to lose tenants to newer and more attractive schemes the owners too often give up hope and watch their investment deteriorate into a transient's hotel.

ARCHITECTURAL FOLLIES IN AMERICA

Not so with the owners of 1211 North LaSalle in Chicago. In 1980 they took their undistinguished block and painted it—not just slapping on a coat and a promise but creating a complete architectural fantasy out of a blank side wall, adding bay windows and a huge Romanesque-arched entrance, flanked by portraits of Chicago School architects Wright, Root, Burnham, and someone who looks like Lenin but who turns out to be Sullivan, all in a wonderfully elaborate three-dimensional trompe l'oeil effect. The transformation took three months and cost $65,000. The artist was Richard Haas, and within a year legends had already sprung up: pigeons were seen trying to land on the nonexistent ledges and a lady was determined to rent the apartment with bay windows.

It's hard to retrace one's steps. I was sent a postcard of the World Famous Upside-Down House built by Norman Johnson at Sunrise Golf Village, Florida—no further information. No one I spoke to in Florida seemed to have heard of it. No one knew of the Sunrise Golf Village. The postcard showed an upside-down bungalow resting on its pitched roof, and a carport with an upside-down 1962 Chrysler glued to the floor (or roof). This was a commercial advertising gimmick and therefore not a folly, but fun to see nevertheless. I had completed an interesting and rather exhausting day in west-central Miami and Opa-Locka and was driving across the state in torrential rain toward the comfort of my hotel, when I saw a sign on the freeway: Sunrise Next Exit. It had not occurred to me that Sunrise was the name of a community. Reader, I hesitated. But I drove on. Is the Upside-Down House still there? World fame is such a transient accolade.

Size is not the only way to attract attention. At different times both Edna Saint Vincent Millay and John Barrymore lived in 75½ Bedford Street, a house in Greenwich Village, New York City, which was claimed to be a mere seven and a half feet wide, but which is nearer nine and a half. This was not the narrowest house in Manhattan. That title was held by the now demolished Spite House, a building of remarkable dimensions and even more remarkable history. The world is a poorer place without a man like Joseph Richardson, mainly because he took as much of it as he could with him. His meanness was legendary. An English immigrant, he made a fortune of $20 million building tenements in New York City, yet a newspaper obituary commented that "throughout his life he has practiced the most rigid economy." He brown-bagged his lunch, he dressed as a hod carrier to plead poverty and so get a doctor's bill reduced from fifty to twenty-five dollars, and all in all came across as a most unpleasant fellow. But in one year, 1882, his miserliness transcended ornery cussedness to become a paeon of premeditated nastiness. Richardson owned a tiny parcel of land, only five feet wide, along the side of Lexington Avenue, between 82nd and 83rd Streets. The developer of an apartment block on 82nd offered Richardson $1,000 for the near worthless strip, which would enable his new building to front Lexington. Richardson demanded $5,000. Horrified, the developer withdrew, and began construction of his new block five feet back from the avenue, with windows overlooking it. Richardson was not only a builder, he was a quick one. Within six months he had built two four-story houses on that five-foot-wide strip, completely shutting out the view from the 82nd Street block. Pure spite, and so naturally the development became known as the Spite House. Once the thickness of the brick construction was taken into account, the rooms were only 3 feet, 4 inches wide. Building regulations permitted bay windows to overhang the lot, so that increased some of the interior space to an expansive 7 feet, 3 inches. Unfortunately for lovers of a good grudge, the Spite House was torn down in 1915.

Rumors of a housing estate built for Hollywood midget actors persisted throughout the research for this book. The rumor was finally nailed down to La Jolla, California, where we found the Munchkin Houses, built on exclusive Hillside Drive. Alas, the rumors proved to be without foundation, rather like the houses themselves, which are perched on struts on the side of Mount Soledad looking out over Torrey Pines Beach. They are perfectly normal bungalows, unobtrusive as you drive up the narrow winding hill, but when you drive back down the reason for the legends becomes clearer. When seen from above the ordinary houses are transformed into picturesque little medleys of broad and low-pitched red pantiled roofs, with deep eaves providing shelter from the hot summer sun. The size of the roofs gives the illusion that the walls are lower than they should be, but an illusion is all it is. No Munchkins danced out to greet us, only full-size Dobermans. The houses were built in 1938 by Cliff May, a popular Southern California architect of the time, in an adapted adobe style. The houses followed the contours of the site rather than obliterating it, giving a rustic, informal effect. The next year *The Wizard of Oz* was released, the world was introduced to the Munchkins, and somehow we weren't in Kansas any more. Neither were the prices: in 1994 one of these houses was valued at $1.5 million.

And finally there is a house in Shepherdstown, West Virginia, that is unexceptional in almost every way. It is a pleasant detached house, solidly built from blue limestone, with two chimneys and three dormer windows in its slate gambrel roof, all very agreeable but nothing out of the ordinary, one might think from looking at a photograph. The reality comes as a surprise. The house is only ten feet high, absolutely perfect for Munchkins. It was built in 1928 to the designs of Florence Shaw, a teaching supervisor at Shepherd College. Not only was the house child-sized, but it was built by children, under the eye of a carpenter and a master stonemason. It began life simply as a summer project to teach children the basics of farming (there is a barn to the same scale) but luckily the idea of the world's largest doll's house took unshakeable root in Miss Shaw's mind and we have been left with this little jewel.

Chapter 3

GORGEOUS PALACES

astles and palaces both suggest lords, monarchs, tyrants, and princesses. The castle is the fortified seat of the warlord, the local despot with the surrounding populace in thrall; robber barons, wicked sheriffs, an evil hegemony blighting the principality. A palace is the paperback edition of a castle; still the seat of absolute power over its subject people, it has a softer outline, a positive image carefully tailored by great public relations men such as Hans Christian Andersen and the brothers Grimm. People who lived in castles wore steel suits, people who lived in palaces wore fancy dress. Palaces are products of leisure and assured control, while castles are paranoid refuges of power. But quite evidently there is no folly in building a castle if your enemies oppress you; equally obviously the construction of a mighty fortress set in a suburban street, where the biggest threat is likely to be the IRS, will inevitably have an air of unreality.

What is not surprising, if you stop and think about it, is that castle building in medieval Europe was carefully monitored and controlled. It is after all a latently aggressive act, like carrying a large gun. You may argue that you have only built it for self defense, but other people may read your motives differently. In twelfth-century England, a gentleman called Hubert de Burgh built himself a castle on the border with Wales. The Welsh were a pretty fearsome lot and no doubt poor Hubert just wanted to guard against a mishap. But he had omitted to apply for a license to crenellate, in other words, permission to build a castle. The Welsh government objected, and the English parliament, which had just concluded a treaty with Wales that forbade the building of any fortifications along the border zone, was forced to order de Burgh to demolish his castle. It was duly written up in Latin in the record books as *Stultitiam Hubertus*, or Hubert's Folly, the first recorded use of the word to describe a building.

Incidentally the English law that demanded a license to crenellate before allowing anyone to add castellations to his house was only repealed this century, after years of disuse.

People in Europe had largely stopped building castles to any great extent by the end of the seventeenth century, and the frontiersmen then colonizing America had no time for fancy stonework—forts and stockades were thrown up in wood, the most readily available material. So the American castle as a genuine headquarters fortified for offense and defense scarcely existed.

This was an omission that a surprising number of people set out to rectify. If America had no real castles, it was ripe to receive some fake ones. Fire a shotgun at a map of the U.S., and where each pellet lands you will find a castellated mansion. Not all of them are castles; some are not follies. The longest surviving castle is an agreeable house cum museum in Brownsville, Pennsylvania, built by Jacob Bowman in 1789. There had previously been a fort on the site where Bowman decided to build his trading post, so it was almost appropriate to call the subsequent house a castle, but just in case anyone questioned the appellation Bowman added an octagonal castellated turret and a castellated façade. Bowman lived in his Nemacolin Castle, which he named after a local Indian chief, for more than fifty years.

One shining exception is Fort Jefferson, a colossal fortress built on Garden Key in the Dry Tortugas, seventy miles beyond Key West in Florida, to protect and control the Gulf of Mexico. It is a near perfect folly, huge, ruinously expensive, atrociously planned, and virtually useless, except it was built by a government rather than an individual. Before air conditioning and pesticides, the Florida Keys were not only unpleasant to live in, they were also inimical to health. In 1846 construction began, and problems beset the enterprise from the start. Conditions were quite simply appalling, supplies were erratic, and after ten years the builders discovered that the weight of the structure was causing it to sink. They had built it on sand shell rather than coral rock. Come the Civil War and Emancipation, the work force disappeared. Prison labor had to be used instead. The penalty for desertion in the Union Army was death; when that was felt to be insufficiently severe, miscreants were sentenced to help build Fort Jefferson. This was America's own Devil's Island, and its completion coincided with a lull in local wars. The garrison stared listlessly out to sea, nothing to see, nothing to do, no escape from the terrible heat, no fresh water except that which was shipped in. Even the army has its limits, and in 1884 it reached them and abandoned the fort. Joy Williams summed up the fort's position in precisely two words: "almost nowhere."

There is, or was, another genuine castle in the shape of a star, buried on the Hawaiian island of Kauai. In 1817 a German adventurer named Georg Anton Scheffer landed on Kauai on a mission to claim the islands for the Czar of Russia. The first thing he did was to construct this fort in a traditional Slavic defensive star pattern, naming it Fort Elizabeth after the Czar's daughter. Alas, this charming gesture failed to interest the Czar, whose attentions were turning north to Alaska, so Scheffer abandoned his fort and wandered off to newer adventures. Fort Elizabeth is still just there, but it is no longer recognizable as such. Curiously shaped mounds of vegetation betray its presence; not a brick or stone can be seen.

The first American castle that could justifiably be called a folly was Edwin Forrest's Fonthill, designed by Thomas L. Smith and begun in New York's Bronx in 1848. Fonthill was the name of a megalomaniac folly in England, perhaps the largest ever built, which collapsed in 1825. Whether the name Fonthill had been chosen in jest or coincidence, we do not know, but Edwin and Catherine Forrest had a copy of *The Delineations of Fonthill Abbey* in their library, and it was clearly used as inspiration for the interior decorations. Forrest was America's first superstar, a high, fine, and handsome actor. William Winter described him as "a vast animal, bewildered by a grain of genius." He is best remembered for his rivalry with the English actor William Macready; passions between the two actors' camps ran so high that in 1849 a riot broke out at the Astor Place Opera House in New York in which twenty-two of Forrest's fans were killed. This was not a great period in Forrest's life. Shortly after buying his beautiful site on the shores of the Hudson River, where he intended that Fonthill's castle walls should "reach down almost to the water's edge," he discovered that the Hudson River Railroad had bought a narrow strip of land along the riverside. The railroad would run through the middle of the house. Forrest theatrically refused compensation—"No money can pay me for the damage you do to me"—and moved the proposed house to higher ground. That same spring he discovered his wife in the arms of another actor and sued for divorce. Catherine countersued, the case dragged on for eighteen years, and she eventually won. So Forrest lost both his loves; he sold his folly to the Sisters of Charity of Saint Vincent de Paul in 1856. Fonthill, still in wonderful condition, is now the library of the College of Mount Saint Vincent.

That is not the only Fonthill in America. A bizarre exterior does not begin to prepare you for the extraordinary interior of another Fonthill, built in Doylestown, Pennsylvania, between 1908 and 1910, by Dr. Henry C. Mercer, sometime curator of American arche- ology at the University of Pennsylvania. Mercer was a true original. He believed that the human eye was a better judge of horizontals and verticals than any spirit level or plumb line, which accounts for the extraordinary shimmering quality of his castle. Mercer was truly a man of his time, highly intelligent, passionate in his enthusiasms, very widely traveled and comfortably well off. He was ideal folly- building material. All he lacked was a very large inheritance to give him more than enough money for his needs. This was provided for by the death of a favorite aunt in 1905. Now seriously rich, Mercer bought land in Doylestown in 1907 that included the Thierolf farm-house. Here he planned his castle, built from the inside out in that he planned the rooms first, then added them to the building as and where he chose. He chose not to demolish the old farmhouse, with the result that it can still be seen swaddled in concrete, peering out from behind three mighty concrete arches. And all around a fanta-sy of windows and staircases and chimneys and concrete roofs swelled and grew. He was impassioned by concrete—a sullen, insipid material that inspires a fiery devotion among its followers—and also by tiles, a more understandable passion. The concrete was laid by eight workers and a horse named Lucy, each of which was paid $1.25 a day. Being unfamiliar with the construction material, the workers and Mercer solved problems on the spot as they arose, with Mercer enthusing about a new and potentially fatal method of tiling ceilings. Electricity was installed, but Mercer disliked the harsh light it gave out, and so designed his next building in Doylestown, a gigantic seven-storied museum, without it. Here he arranged the windows in an arc to provide the maximum input of light, moving around the building to catch the sun as the day pro-gressed. Power was finally installed (with great difficulty in the solid concrete walls) in the late 1970s. Mercer's passion for tiles and pot-tery was reflected in his pride and joy, the Moravian Pottery and Tileworks, based on the design of a temple in Yucatan or a Spanish hacienda, depending on your point of view.

The original farmhouse peers through three concrete arches at Dr. Mercer's Fonthill.

At the same time that the first Fonthill was being built, a marble palace was rising in upstate New York on the banks of the Hudson, a favorite location for folly builders. Tarrytown, on that wide stretch of the river above Yonkers, was chosen by General William Paulding and his son Philip Paulding, the mayor of New York from 1824 to 1826, as the site for their Gothic Revival mansion of Lyndhurst. Alexander J. Davis, the great country house architect, had planned a two-story marble dwelling of no more than a dozen rooms, well endowed with buttresses and crocketed pinnacles, but still not much more than a villa. There was little of the folly about it, although the Gothic Revival style was still recent and unusual enough to excite comment. But all politicians attract their opponents and Philip Hone was particularly vindictive: "an edifice of gigantic size, with no room in it; great cost and little comfort, which, if I mistake not, will one of these days be designated as Paulding's Folly."

A.k.a. Paulding's Folly and Merrit's Folly, the gloriously Gothic Lyndhurst doesn't deserve that vindictive assessment.

Not until George Merrit, a New York merchant, bought the property in 1864, did it really begin to live up to that name. Alexander Davis, whose reputation was then at its peak, had recently completed Castle Herrick nearby, full blown with castellations, turrets, and towers (but sadly demolished in 1944), so Merrit employed him to come back and enlarge the house, adding a new tower and virtually doubling its size. Merrit had not finished, and photographs of what he next achieved make one gasp in wonder. He landscaped twenty acres of park and built an absolutely gigantic greenhouse, the biggest in the world, with a 100-foot glass tower in the middle, surmounted by a glass onion dome.

Merrit died in 1873, and his magnificent folly fell into decay. Then a real robber baron stepped in. Jay Gould, the unscrupulous railroad tycoon, bought the estate in 1880. Lyndhurst, a.k.a. Paulding's Folly and Merrit's Folly (so good they named it twice), stayed in the Gould family until 1961. The National Trust for Historic Preservation took it over in 1964, a folly in names alone.

We have no record of how Alexander Davis felt about hearing his handiwork at Lyndhurst referred to as Paulding's Folly. He was prepared for eclecticism: in his diary he noted (with, we must infer, a touch of pride) that he could design houses in a variety of styles, including "American Log Cabin, Frame House, English Cottage, Collegiate Gothic Manor House, French Suburban, Switz Cottage, Lombard Italian, Tuscan from Pliny's Villa at Ostia, Ancient Etruscan, Suburban Greek, Oriental, Moorish and Castellated." Calvert Vaux, however, must have anticipated the sobriquet sticking to his Belvedere Castle, a splendidly romantic piece of sham Gothickery built in 1872 and conceived by the great landscape architect Frederick Law Olmsted purely as a lookout and an adornment to New York's Central Park.

Vaux's Belvedere Castle is a splendidly romantic adornment to New York's Central Park.

ARCHITECTURAL FOLLIES IN AMERICA

Twenty-three years later a genuine New York castle loomed over Madison Avenue, between 94th and 95th Streets on the Upper East Side. What remains today is just the wall of the Squadron A Armory; a real castle wall but now without a castle. The armory was erected in 1895 to the designs of John Rochester Thomas in a brutal, frowning castle style as befits an armory, taking up the entire block. But by 1966, the need for a school was greater than the need for a castle. It was to be torn down; but the public had grown accustomed to the Armory's face, and a campaign was launched to save it. The school, designed by Morris Ketchum Jr., now neatly incorporates the Madison Avenue façade of the old armory as the playground wall, and the castle, once real, has become fairy tale.

Still in New York City, Francis Bannerman's emporium of antique weaponry stood on the edge of Greenwich Village at 501 Broadway, but the premises were not large enough to house the company's massive stock. A warehouse was required, but why make do with a tedious large shed when there were much more exciting possibilities? In 1900 Bannerman bought Pollepel Island in the Hudson River, just south of Beacon, and there he erected a mammoth proto-folly, a wild, exuberant explosion of architectural styles as if Mayan Indians had once seen a picture of a Scottish baronial castle, then tried to build it from memory. It cannot be seen from the road, but train commuters will know it well. Bannerman's arsenal had everything the young knight dreaming of glory could want—towers, castellations, docks, and vast quantities of weapons and explosives; a thought to gladden every hero's heart.

The Tampa Bay Hotel in Florida is not a castle, not a palace, more an alcazar, and it is now used partly by the University of Tampa and partly by the Henry B. Plant Museum. Opened by the railroad magnate Plant in 1891 for the then staggering cost of $3 million, which was recouped through rooms costing as much as $75 a night, the hotel was a huge success during the age of the grand hotel, but the Depression proved too much for it and it closed in 1929. Such an astonishing piece of architecture—built of concrete reinforced with railroad ties and inspired by the Alhambra in Spain with its remarkable roof line of six tin-sheathed, onion-domed minarets, four cupolas, and three domes—could not be allowed to perish, and it was bought by the university in 1933. A recent restoration has returned the old dowager to her former splendor.

Not all castles have to be mighty edifices frowning from distant hills. In the latter half of the nineteenth century, twin castles were built by brothers in Ohio, stony expressions of sibling rivalry with suitably enigmatic names. Col. Don Piatt, a newspaper proprietor and Civil War soldier, built Mac-O-Chee Castle just to the east of West Liberty as a copy of a French chateau, while his brother built Mac-A-Cheek Castle, a couple of miles to the south. Aberdeen, Mississippi, had a tiny toylike, L-shaped wooden castle, small but perfectly formed with gable battlements, three castellated towers of various sizes, and formal window moldings, built by a Mr. de Courcy in 1884; a caparisoned cottage. For some reason this entrancing gem failed to satisfy a later owner who, in 1937, had all the character of the house obliterated by removing two of the towers and a bay window and adding a distinctly unsympathetic bungalow-style porch along the length of the façade. Utter desecration.

Feargus Squire made his fortune through oil, retiring in 1909 as general manager of Standard Oil, the forerunner of Exxon. In the 1890s, struck by the beauty of the Chagrin Valley outside Cleveland, Ohio, he bought a 525-acre parcel of land with the intention of turning it into his country estate. The main house was inspired by a high German baronial hall, the gatehouse by an English castle. Paths, roads, lakes, bridges, and woods were scattered over the estate. The gatehouse was built, the family spent weekends there, but as time dragged on there was still no sign of the high baronial hall. By the time Squire reached seventy-two, it was fairly obvious that nothing was going to happen, so the property was sold and became a public park in 1925. Squire's Castle still stands as a roofless, shattered wreck, a gatehouse to folly.

We can mourn the palaces and castles we have lost, but some are better gone than forgotten. Sen. William A. Clark, the "Montana Copper King," built an alarmingly overweight granite house in Manhattan on the corner of Fifth Avenue and 77th Street, the sort of building that would wear blue polyester stretch pants if it were human, adorned with a $400,000 copper roof that doubled the sale of sunglasses in the area before oxidization mercifully lessened the glare. It had everything: 130 rooms including the mandatory theater and ballroom, a gigantic tower, elaborate crestings, every imaginable type of stone carving, cartouche, decoration, and ornament— but was it pure folly? Clark managed to get his New York City property taxes reduced by hundreds of thousands of dollars on the grounds that the $6 million palace was so individual that few would buy it. He was right. Nobody bought it, and it was demolished after his death.

Still standing on West 44th Street in Manhattan is the New York Yacht Club, built in 1900 by the firm of Warren and Wetmore. It may not be a folly, as it has served as a comfortable clubhouse for the great and the good for the best part of a century, but the grand windows overlooking the street are whimsical in the extreme—the sterns of three mighty galleons sailing up to Central Park, hopefully to dock at the Belvedere Castle.

George Boldt, a Prussian immigrant, tasted failure and success in huge measures. He failed to cut it as a chicken farmer. Sheep farming was no better, but transposed to the New York hotel business he shot to stardom, acquiring the patronage of William Waldorf Astor, who backed him in a speculative enterprise. When Boldt's new hotel, the Waldorf, opened in 1893, he had thirty-two guests. The hotel was quickly dubbed Boldt's Folly, but Boldt persevered in the face of adversity and through titanic hard work the Waldorf became the flagship of New York hotels, making Boldt a very rich man. The Astoria followed shortly afterwards, along with hotels and clubs in Philadelphia. Nor was this Boldt's Folly. George did not do things by halves. So when he fell in love nothing was to be too good for his Louise. Together they fell in love with the Thousand Islands in the Saint

The sterns of three mighty galleons anchor the grand windows of the New York Yacht Club.

Lawrence River, incidentally perpetrating Thousand Island Dressing, and George built a castle for his princess. He bought Hart Island and built an artificial embankment to change the shape of the island, allowing him to rechristen it Heart Island. This was just the beginning. For two years Boldt's workmen labored with Prussian speed; a castle arose, an Arc de Triomphe, a tower, a powerhouse, all in a heavy Rhenish Gothic with huge rusticated stonework. The complexity was astonishing; the plan had evidently been fermenting in Boldt's mind for ages. Eleven buildings were planned, with the main castle designed to accommodate one hundred guests, together with their servants. This was entertaining on an Astorian scale, and ballrooms, bedrooms, billiard rooms, and bathrooms were poured into the great building.

This was a dream commission for the architects, Hewitt, Stevens, and Paist of Philadelphia. When clients specify work, there are three main considerations: speed, price, and quality. To get any two one has to compromise on the third. Boldt compromised. "The price will be immaterial," he barked. By 1902 the whole astounding pro-

After receiving news of his beloved wife's death, George Boldt halted work on his rusticated-stonework castle.

ject was nearing completion. Opulent furnishings were being imported from Europe: fireplaces, chandeliers, paintings, tapestries. Then in January came the telegram. Louise Boldt was dead. Work stopped immediately, never to be resumed. George, heartbroken, never revisited his Taj Mahal on Heart Island.

A different love lay behind the construction of the three Searles castles. Edward F. Searles was working for Herter Brothers, a famous firm of interior decorators in New York City, when, in 1882, he went to San Francisco to visit Mary, the widow of the railroad tycoon Mark Hopkins, to look at her collection of antique furniture. Something about the handsome, six foot, forty-two-year-old confirmed bachelor appealed to the rich widow, twenty-one years his senior, and soon she asked him to supervise the construction of a mansion she was planning to build in Great Barrington, Massachusetts. McKim, Mead and White were the original architects, but it was not long before Searles took over and acted as Mrs. Hopkins's superintendent, architect, and financial and confidential adviser. Searles was surprised to discover he was not going to be paid his usual 10 percent commission, but remarked astutely, "I thought I would be paid in the end, some way." And so he was; in 1887 he and Mary were married. The mansion, then known as Kellogg Terrace, was completed in 1888. Together they then built a million-dollar mansion on Block Island, Rhode Island, which was occupied for two months then abandoned. They bought another mansion at 60 Fifth Avenue in New York City. Four years of nuptial bliss came to an end when Mrs. Searles died at Searles's own home in Methuen, Massachusetts, amid rumors of skullduggery, leaving her entire estate to her young bridegroom, bar $10 million or so to her adopted son, who naturally enough contested the will. Edward Searles, feeling that his reward was adequate for nine years' hard work, won the case and bought a thousand acres of New Hampshire, thirty miles north of Boston.

Searles was a man of mercurial temperament, willful, with an undeserved reputation of starting projects but not finishing them, and a rather cruel streak that made him want things only because other people wanted them. At first a degree of modesty prevailed and he built a one-room cottage on his New Hampshire acres, but then realizing he was richer than any nineteenth-century interior decorator was ever likely to be, he went in at the deep end and built himself a castle. He allegedly had the design based on Stanton Harcourt Manor in Oxfordshire, England. Irving Vaughan, his archi-

Edwin Searles inherited millions, bought a thousand acres in New Hampshire, and built himself a castle.

tect, went to England to make a measured drawing of the castle, but found it had been pulled down in the eighteenth century. Only Pope's Tower, a small portion of the whole, remained, and the only similarity between it and Searles Castle at Windham is that they both have castellations. Searles just carried on building, anything and anywhere. He built three schools in Great Barrington and Methuen, a church in Windham, New Hampshire. He adorned his

The granite water tower at Searles' Pine Lodge estate serves equally well as a monstrous garden ornament.

hometown with two churches, a Masonic temple, a bridge, and a music hall. At Pine Lodge, his estate in Methuen, he built a massive four-square granite tower, rather worryingly perched on the side of a hill rather than at the top, which served equally well as a monstrous garden ornament and a water tower. Persistent vandalism means the tower is now threatened with condemnation. When Searles died in 1920 he left a fortune of more than $50 million to his sec-

Things have
never quite
worked out for
Evans Dick's
Moorish-style
castle—
unoccupied and
incomplete after
ninety years.

retary and companion, Arthur T. Walker, a huge sum even after three decades of incessant building. Searles Castle in Great Barrington is now a school for delinquent boys, Searles Castle in Methuen houses the convent of the Sisters of the Preservation of Mary, and the Sisters of Mercy own Searles Castle in Windham.

The wife of Evans R. Dick developed a taste for Moorish architecture. Enough said. Dick, a New York financier, dispatched an architect to Spain to study the Moorish style and bought several large chunks of land in Garrison-on-Hudson, New York. From the top of a 410-foot hill the most astounding 20-mile panoramic views could be had, and it was here that Dick decided to build his castle. The cost was estimated at $7 million, the equivalent of over $50 million today, and construction rambled on for seven years until 1911, when Dick's business faltered and a halt was finally called. Half the budget had been spent, and the place was still nowhere near finished—for a start there were no internal walls. There was an 86-foot tower, one wing stretched out for 180 feet, another for 220 feet, and there was really no point to it at all. For the Dick family it was the end of the line, and the unoccupied palace stood unfinished until 1944 when a radio manufacturer, Anton Chmela, bought it with the intention of turning it into a factory. A year later the war ended, and Chmela's visions of huge profits danced out the window. Still the castle stood empty. Finally, in the mid-1950s, Chmela bowed to the demands of his family, made one floor of one wing habitable and moved in. At last, after fifty years, the castle had its first tenants, even though they occupied less than a tenth of the total floor space. Heating rooms 100 feet long throughout a New York winter can be an expensive undertaking. Chmela's daughter Helen and her family lived there until 1979 when they sold it to the Dia Art Foundation, which wanted to use the castle as a gallery. Things didn't work out, so Dia sold it to a group of local investors. Things didn't work out, so the group of local investors sold it to the Moorish Castle Corporation in 1988. Things again didn't work out, so the Moorish Castle Corporation put it up for auction in 1994, after spending $5 million in an attempt to complete it. At the time it had been independently valued at $16.8 million, and the auction reserve was a mere $4.8 million. It was and is a sensational building, white walled and red roofed in the thick green forest, with those amazing views over the Hudson. A visit in the summer of 1993 revealed an apparently complete but totally unfurnished palace, marble floors and mahogany framed windows, sparkling new with weeds vigorously thrusting their way up in the courtyards. After ninety years Dick's Castle, currently called Garrison Hall, remains unoccupied and incomplete. This is a huge and spectacular folly.

The only example of cereal architecture I've ever found is in South Dakota, where the Corn Palaces rise above the corn-clad prairie year after year after year. In 1890 the small town of Plankinton, South Dakota, celebrated a bumper harvest by erecting a Grain Palace. Alarm and despondency filled the citizens of Mitchell, twenty-odd miles away, as they conferred as to how they might counter this threat from a rival community. Louis Beckwith proposed a Corn Palace, and in 1892 Mitchell's citizens built a meeting hall with turrets along each side and a central tower, which they proceeded to envelop in split corn and grain in a kaleidoscope of patterns. Plankinton was blown away, and within ten years Mitchell was in the running for the state capital. Pierre finally won that race, but by then the citizen's passions were concentrated on their ever more elaborately decorated Corn Palace. In 1904 Mitchell, this small town in the middle of nowhere, tried to book the John Philip Sousa band, the biggest name in entertainment, to play at their annual Corn Palace Festival. Sousa's manager laughed and quoted an outrageous $7,000

The world's largest bird feeder, the Corn Palace in Mitchell, South Dakota, gets a new cereal cladding every September. (This view is from an old postcard.)

fee. Mitchellers pursed their lips and agreed. When Sousa arrived, he took one look at the unpaved Main Street and refused to get off the train until he was given a check for the full fee. The town paid in cash. Sousa ended up giving an extra concert each day of the festival, and coming back for a repeat performance three years later. A second Corn Palace, much bigger, with minarets and conical-roofed towers, was built in 1905 to replace the first, and a tradition of booking big name entertainment for the festival had begun. By 1919 the second Corn Palace was too small, and a third, larger, plainer building was planned. But the native exuberance of the South Dakotan could not be restrained and ten years later the plain Corn Palace III had acquired domes, cupolas, and minarets. And so the Corn Palaces have grown and prospered, making Mitchell the most famous little city in South Dakota. There is of course only one Corn Palace, but each year it is bedecked with more than 3,000 bushels of colored corn and grain to form giant murals on the walls and on the Moorish domes and turrets of the basic building. The decorations, largely in natural colors and grown locally, cost about $40,000 each year. The time to see the Corn Palace is at the end of September, just after the new decorations have been applied and shortly before the palace takes on its annual role as the world's largest bird feeder. Corn siding is no substitute for aluminum.

ARCHITECTURAL FOLLIES IN AMERICA

Castles and palaces are fleshed out by an infusion of monarchy. A much-traveled man from the West Coast, Sam Hill, made his fortune from railroads and highways with projects in America, Russia, and Japan. He attended a university in Munich, Germany, where his roommate turned out to be the Crown Prince of Belgium. Any sensible man would have kept in touch, and Sam was sensible. His fortune made, he built a castle in Seattle and invited Prince Albert to stay. Alas, King Leopold died and the Prince was unable to come. Undeterred, Sam built another, bigger, better castle in the Flemish style four years later on the Columbia River which he called Maryhill, while everyone else who saw it called it Sam Hill's Folly. Again he invited the prince, now the king, to stay. Unfortunately, at the same time, the German army decided to go and stay in Belgium, making it difficult for the new king to leave. Finally, in frustration Sam turned his castle into a museum, at which point Queen Marie of Romania turned up and left her regalia there, saying it would be much safer with Sam than in Europe. Given the subsequent history of that unhappy country, it was a prescient act.

Seventh Sister in Hadlyme, Connecticut, now better known as Gillette Castle, was built in 1914 by William C. Gillette—not the Razor King, but a hugely successful actor of his time—and was

No fortress on the Rhine ever looked like Gillette Castle, in Hadlyme, Connecticut.

allegedly based on a Rhenish castle. He chose the hill, the Seventh Sister, for its spectacular views. No castle on the Rhine ever looked like this, neither does anything else. Ragged in outline and built from huge random blocks of pale local granite, the castle glitters in the sunlight, its latticed, sporadic fenestration shaded by stone icicles or savage teeth. Naturally, Gillette was his own architect; if one building can be said to be the expression of the will of one man, this is it. His pride and joy was the three-mile private steam railroad running through the grounds, from his own Grand Central Station, but Gillette had barely shuffled off his last stage before the tracks were torn up in direct contradiction of his will and sold to an amusement park in Lake Compounce. Displayed on a wall of the castle is a copy of his will, a fascinating document too long to be quoted here and too embarrassing to be quoted in official histories. One phrase has passed into the public domain—Gillette knew full well that the world was full of "blithering sapheads," and he was at pains to ensure that his magnificent estate should not fall into the hands of people who would not be able to appreciate it, and in particular that his railroad should be well cared for. The sapheads won, although to be fair the castle is excellently preserved and looked after, and the only major loss is the railroad. But what a loss.

More than a thousand workers labored to build James Deering's tastefully eclectic Florida palace, Vizcaya.

The warm, sunny climes of Florida and California are ideal for fruits and nuts. Palaces also thrive well, with four major examples blossoming in the early twentieth century. On Biscayne Bay to the south of Miami, James Deering initiated work in 1912 on a medieval Venetian palace which he called Vizcaya, after the Spanish for Biscayne. Deering had made his money by merging the Deering Harvester Company, the company his father founded, into the International Harvester Company, becoming a multimillionaire in the process. He spent it, and, being a bachelor, had no heirs to resent it. He suffered from ill-health and was advised to seek a warm climate. At a time when the population of Miami was less than 10,000, he employed more than 1,000 to build his palace. The style of the house was originally intended to be Spanish—hence the name—but Deering fell under the spell of his autocratic artistic supervisor Paul Chalfin, who wrote implacably, "we came to the determination that the building should be of the Italian villa type." Vizcaya is a rectangular building with a fifteenth-century façade facing the waterfront, a sixteenth-century north façade, a seventeenth-century garden façade, and an eighteenth-century entrance front. This is not a pastiche of half-remembered architectural themes; it is a scholarly,

ARCHITECTURAL FOLLIES IN AMERICA

some may say arrogant, reassembly of existing periods and motifs, yet somehow it all works, it all blends together in tasteful eclecticism. It gives the impression that the original house had been remodeled over the centuries as time, taste, and money permitted, as was the case with so many of the grand houses of Europe. We have now reached an era when we lack the confidence to be able to rebuild portions of an existing grand house in a contemporary style; even if we had the confidence we would not get the consent.

One may feel that there is sufficient eccentricity in building a house that stylistically spans four centuries, but the great joy at Vizcaya as far as we are concerned lies offshore. During construction and the dredging of the hammock, as the native forest out of which Vizcaya grew is called, a number of small islets were formed, and there was some worry that these would be claimed by the state, thus ceasing to be part of the property. Chalfin's garden designer Diego Suarez provided the solution. He had visited the Lago Maggiore in the north of Italy, in which lies the fantastic *Isola Bella* "Beautiful Island," which has been remade in its entirety into the shape of a ship. Suarez took the largest of the Vizcaya islets and devised a great breakwater in the form of a stately ceremonial barge, apparently moored just offshore. The barge was carved out of coral stone by Stirling Calder at a cost of $8,000, a sum that Deering resented as he felt the carvings would be coarse. It is a triumph of garden architecture.

Ten years later and two hundred miles away on the east coast of the state rose another Venetian palace, John and Mable Ringling's Ca'd'Zan in Sarasota. There was more concern here for chronological authenticity, the Ringlings preferring to choose one particular architectural period and stick to it. As a result, their 1924 palace looks as if it had been built in Venice in 1492; whether they decided on such an anagrammatic date as a joke (they were circus folk, after all) or to commemorate a certain sea voyage undertaken that year is not known. Their architect, Dwight J. Baum, had proposed a Georgian-style house, but the Ringlings had their hearts set on Venetian Gothic. The House of John (Ca'd'Zan, in the Venetian dialect) rose in multicolored magnificence facing due east on the Sarasota shore, its perfect alignment emphasized by a large mosaic compass set in a path in front of the house. Later Baum professionally retreated from such polychromatic splendor and went on to reach fortune and fame from more conventional structures, but the eccentric beauty of Ca'd'Zan remains his best-loved work.

The multicolored magnificence of Ca'd'Zan suited the taste of the circus folk who built it.

A man's expression of love for his wife can take many forms. Shah Jahan enshrined his grief at losing his wife Mumtaz in the exquisite beauty of the Taj Mahal; Irwin A. Yarnell built a castle for his living, loving wife. La Casa de Josefina cost $1.5 million to build in 1923, an uncertain combination of Gothic, Spanish, and Italian architecture—anyway, lots of turrets and castellations—set on a bare rolling hill south of Lake Wales, Florida. It does appear that Josefina appreciated the gesture, for despite family tragedies including the loss of a son and a daughter and a downturn in the family fortunes after the death of Irwin, she held on to the property until she died in 1968, by closing wings, selling off jewelry, taking in boarders, and renting part of the castle as a nursing home. After her death the castle drifted from owner to owner until it was bought and restored by Jean Louwsma in 1981. Mrs. Louwsma claims to be an intensely private person, yet she takes journalists on tours of the house, and claims she is living there only to look after it for Josefina.

Josefina Yarnell did everything she could to hold onto the house that her husband had built as a gesture of love.

The William Randolph Hearst story is more like the Bill Gates story than *Citizen Kane*. No rags to riches here; they were both sons of rich men who made themselves even richer. But Citizen Kane's Xanadu could only hint at the torrid grandeur of Hearst Castle, San Simeon, La Casa Grande—so big they named it thrice. Four times, if you count the original name of the property, the Piedra Blanca Ranch, which Hearst's father bought in 1865. Hearst started building on the site, by then known as Camp Hill, in 1919, having employed the prolific San Francisco architect Julia Morgan, an apparently timid, self-effacing woman whose mild exterior concealed a titanium resolve and ability to fabricate extraordinary effects at reasonable prices. Visitors to Berkeley's City Club, which Morgan designed as a women's club in 1929, are swept away by the cloistered charm of mock medievality, cheaply and effectively achieved with poured concrete, molds, and wooden battens. Morgan was married to her work, putting in up to eighteen hours a day, six days a week. It is doubtful that any architect before or since has approached the quantity of her output—more than eight hundred major buildings in the forty-six years she ran her office. Nor was this achieved through delegation: she herself dealt directly with all her clients, from Hearsts to taxi drivers. Perhaps her greatest strength was her ability to interpret their dreams and create them in wood, stone, and concrete. In Hearst she found a dreamer on a colossal scale. It started simply enough. Morgan had worked with Hearst's mother Phoebe on a chain of YWCAs throughout the western states. After Phoebe died in 1919, Hearst approached Morgan about building a place on Camp Hill, saying, "I get tired of going up there and camping in tents. I'm getting a little old for that." He showed her a book of bungalow plans he had unearthed. "Keep it simple," he advised her.

How then did one of the most spectacular palaces in America arise from that modest instruction? Was it Hearst or Morgan who succumbed to megalomania? Walter Steilberg, an architect in Morgan's practice, sketched the first plan, but it was quickly obvious that something grander was going to be required. Hearst already had a remarkable collection of art that included paneled rooms, ceilings, and architectural antiques among paintings and sculptures, and on his mother's death he inherited far more. A bungalow would hardly be adequate to display it. Morgan quickly comprehended her task. "I'm not building a residence, I'm building a museum," she said to her staff. The guest houses came first, with La Casa Del Mar, overlooking the Pacific, being completed within the first year. It was followed the next year by La Casa del Monte, with a view of the Santa Lucia Mountains, and the following year by La Casa del Sol, with a view of the setting sun. These "cottages" had only eighteen or so rooms, and decoration that was merely sensational rather than mind boggling. The Big House was not ready to move into until 1925. By now it was apparent that all this was really something, even by the standards of millionaires, and still another name was given to the site: *la Cuesta Encantada*, "the Enchanted Hill." The indoor swimming pool, known as the Roman Pool, was covered in mosaics that took three and a half years to place. From the architectural salvage Hearst supplied, Morgan created the outdoor Neptune Pool, probably the most lavish ever constructed. Hearst bought more works of art than he could ever hope to handle. Many of his purchases went directly into storage, never to be unpacked. In the end, La Casa Grande was the world's most beautiful warehouse.

We are fortunate that Hearst and Morgan met when they did. Ten years later the 1929 crash ended, perhaps forever, the ability of an individual to build on this scale. Construction did not stop immediately; it slowly ran down until 1937. Plans for additional wings stayed rolled up. The Big House was never finished.

A Wild West legend and a Chicago millionaire teamed up to build Scotty's Castle, in Death Valley, California.

ARCHITECTURAL FOLLIES IN AMERICA

Out in the invigorating if threatening California desert, a strange structure began to rise in Death Valley in 1924. Scotty's Castle is now a well-known tourist destination. But why was it built? Death Valley Scotty, as Walter Perry Scott liked to be known, was an extrovert, if such a mild word can be used for one who used to throw gold nuggets and one-hundred-dollar bills out of train windows, who worked as a bronco buster with Annie Oakley, who hired a train to make a record-breaking run from Los Angeles to Chicago, who prospected for gold unsuccessfully for three years and was consequently chased all over the West by his erstwhile partner. Such men make legends even if they don't always build castles. Scotty did, because he eventually found his gold mine in the shape of one Albert Johnson, a sickly but impressively rich Chicagoan whose health was greatly improved by the clean dry desert air. Johnson built a block house in 1922 on the site, but Scotty hankered after a castle, and Johnson allowed him to have it. Work started in 1927, with two low buildings separated by a central courtyard and a circular tower with an open string spiral staircase at the end of the back block. A large, handsome clock tower with Westminster chimes and a lovely, multicolored tiled, pyramidal roof stood on a low hill to the west, with the longest, loudest sustain of any bell I've heard. Maybe

The bell in the clock tower rings loud and long in the clear desert air.

it's the clear desert air. Frank Lloyd Wright was originally approached to act as the architect, but his designs—"beautiful in their indigenous purity," wrote Johnson—were rejected as not being sufficiently ornate, and they turned to a Los Angeles designer, C. Alexander MacNeilledge. By the spring of 1931, it was all nearing completion. The landscaping was still to be done, including terraced grounds and a tea garden, and the 250-foot serpentine swimming pool merely awaited tiling, but the 1929 crash had hit Johnson hard. He ordered all work to stop, and Scotty had no gold mine to make up the shortfall. In the end the construction cost was more than $2 million, or $4 million, or $10 million, depending on Scotty's mood as he told the story. But despite running out of serious money, both Johnson and Scotty derived huge pleasure from the ranch for many years, until they died in 1948 and 1954 respectively. "He repays me in laughs," said Johnson about his roguish partner. The sprawling, eclectic Spanish Moorish fantasy, 3,000 feet up in Grapevine Canyon, was originally known as the Johnson and Scott Death Valley Ranch, but Scotty's huge personality dominated the entire development and inevitably it has become known as Scotty's Castle. The tiles for the unfinished serpentine swimming pool still remain stored in the castle's basement.

We talked of palaces and princesses at the start, but although we have had a Belgian prince and the Queen of Romania there have been distressingly few princesses so far. In Phoenix, Arizona, Boyce Luther Gulley started to build the Mystery Castle for a princess in 1927, on the foothills of the South Mountain. Gulley was a shoe salesman, and the princess was his daughter Mary Lou. Having

A shoe salesman built Mystery Castle for his daughter—but she never saw it till he died.

abandoned his wife and Mary Lou, he took up with an abandoned box car, then improved it into an 18-room, 8,000-square-foot, sham medieval hacienda, never letting his daughter near the site. From the surrounding fence the original boxcar can no longer be made out under the accretions of the years. A tower with no discernible back tilts queasily toward an arch. Adobe surmounts stone, brick, wood, and wagon wheels. The roof line looks like a temperature chart for downtown Phoenix. Mary Lou saw it for the first time after Gulley died in 1945, moved in and never left. The castle is open to the public six days a week from October to July and closed on Mondays, the day we visited. "I've come from Scottsdale to see this," grumbled a frustrated visitor. Peering through the cyclone fence I thought of home, five thousand miles away, and said nothing.

"There was nothing odd about Harry," mused an old friend of Harry Andrews from Loveland, Ohio, "'cept he built himself a castle." Harry started building Château Laroche on the banks of the Little Miami River in 1929, two years after Gulley began. This was a more traditional affair—stone, brick, and concrete built, four square and castellated—but each stone and brick was put into place by Andrews alone. He was not working from a romantic dream but from an educated understanding of architecture; he had studied Egyptian, Greek, and Roman architecture at Colgate University before going on to postgraduate work in Norman architecture in Toulouse, France. He knew what he was doing, he simply preferred to do it himself. Some of the boys from the Sunday school where he taught helped him, but over the next forty years the greater bulk of the work was carried out single-handedly by Andrews. He made the bricks by filling milk cartons with concrete, built a road to the castle, bored a well, used oil cans covered in concrete to make a damp-proof floor, and solved each problem as he came to it in his own way. Harry was keen on medieval pageantry as well as symbolism; the 88 battlements on the castle stood for the 88 counties of Ohio, and the 50 battlements on the north wing represented the states of the Union. He retired from teaching in 1955 and devoted himself full time to his castle and his boy helpers, the Knights of the Golden Trail. The reward for helping Harry build his castle was to be knighted. According to Harry, he had been knighted on the field of battle in the First World War; history is a little shaky as to how this happened, but the result is that the south of Ohio is awash with knights. Andrews carried on building an underground garage and a retaining wall until he was sadly burned to death in a trash fire in 1981.

ARCHITECTURAL FOLLIES IN AMERICA

The Coral Castle at Homestead, Florida, was a ten-acre romantic dream. It was built single-handedly by a jilted Latvian immigrant, Edward Leedskalnin, as a hopeless tribute to his improbably named ex-fiancée Agnes Scuffs, whom he referred to throughout his life as "Sweet Sixteen." On the eve of their wedding, she jilted him, telling him that at twenty-six he was too old for her. Broken hearted, he fled Latvia and emigrated to Canada. He worked his way down through California and Texas, working variously as a lumberjack and cowboy until he was told he had tuberculosis and was advised to seek a warmer climate. He arrived in Florida just after World War I. Buying an acre of land in Florida City for $12.50, Leedskalnin began to carve the coral rock he found under the thin Florida topsoil. He carved a chair, then a table, then an entire castle. Then he decided to move to Homestead, ten miles away, because Florida City was becoming too crowded. He bought ten acres along U.S. Route 1 and instead of starting over, he singlehandedly and secretively transported his castle, bit by bit, by night to Homestead, leaving just one tower behind. Apparently the plan was that he would become so famous by building this massive rock coral castle that Sweet Sixteen would hear about it in Vilnius and come back to him. He died unfulfilled in 1951, but his romantic dream endures. A father and daughter from New York, visiting on Thanksgiving 1993, were so entranced by the castle that they failed to hear the closing bells. The police and the manager, still picking turkey out of his teeth, arrived to release them, and the father shuffled out: "This is so beautiful, honey, you've got to get married here!" What puzzles visitors is how a small, slight man like Leedskalnin (five feet tall, one hundred pounds) managed to shift and balance these massive rocks, some weighing up to thirty tons. One slab, the Nine Ton Gate, was so perfectly balanced that it swung open or shut at the touch of a finger; was, because it now requires a very hefty shove to move it. Hurricane Andrew, in August 1992, left the Coral Castle virtually untouched, while devastation laid waste all around. It is a remarkable, tormented accomplishment.

It took Harry Andrews forty years to build Château Laroche; he did all the work himself (with a little help from his Sunday school classes).

Jim Bishop bears a startling resemblance to Gene Wilder in *High Anxiety*, but that's about as far as the similarity goes. Bishop is as solid as the castle he is building in Pueblo, Colorado. He is his own master and his own architect, and his dreams are unfettered by formal architectural precedents. Bishop's Castle rewrites the book on defensive medieval architecture. It is a fantastical structure, all arched buttresses and steeply pitched metal roofs assembled from the sides of railroad box cars, a 100-foot tower with a bartizan side turret all built out of massive, rubbly, undressed river rock on a two-acre site. The bartizan turret has a gleaming gold acorn roof, a Colorado Kremlin. On the top of the steeply raked high gable is a dragon's head, mouth agape, designed to spew flames. Bishop started work on the castle in 1969, part time at first but now full time, while his two sons run his metal fabrication shop. The castle has a gift shop, a kitchen, and a living room with a 20-foot ceiling, a museum on the second floor also with a 20-foot ceiling to display the medieval weapons and suits of armor he has collected or created, and the third floor is the ballroom, with a mighty 40-foot ceiling and an organ salvaged from a local church. Why is he doing it? "I've dreamed of building a castle since I was a kid. I got hooked on the idea. It tugged at me until 1969, when I decided to do something about it." Bishop enjoys dressing as a knight in homemade armor and posing with his battle-ax in front of his castle. It seems a shame he chose to locate his castle in Colorado in preference to Maryland, where the official state sport is jousting.

No wonder Solomon's castle shimmers in the moonlight: it's clad in aluminum printing plates.

Knight, bishop, castle—the link has already been made by Howard Solomon. Buried in the backwoods between Arcadia and Ona in central Florida is a glittering silver castle with towers,

ARCHITECTURAL FOLLIES IN AMERICA

portcullis, castellations, and a moat complete with full-size wooden galleon. It is the creation of a sculptor, New York State–born Solomon, who claims his family have been unemployed castle builders for four centuries. He decided to do something about it. Solomon is a serious artist who is unable to take himself seriously. He has been recycling unlikely materials into sculptures and buildings since way before recycling became the norm. His life-size sculpture of a horse, made out of wire coat hangers, is displayed in Ripley's Believe It or Not museum in Saint Augustine. The reason his castle shines so radiantly in the sunlight—or indeed the moonlight, when it takes on a breathtaking fairytale aspect—is that the basic wooden structure is clad with aluminum litho printing plates that he bought as scrap from the local newspaper for ten cents a sheet. "Now that they've found out what I'm doing with them they're charging me thirty-five cents a plate—oy!" You can never be sure when Solomon is joking. He owns a lot of the land around, and his castle sits in one corner acre of a 64-acre lot. On the adjacent acres he is planning to build a gigantic knight, then a bishop . . .

A castle that is not a castle lifts its battlements above the wind-torn trees on Saint Augustine's North Beach in Florida. A sign on the gate reads "Castle Otttis. An Original Sculpture Done in Remembrance of Jesus Christ." Well, this is not a sculpture, it is a building, and one that looks a lot like a castle at that. It was built by two men, Rusty Ickes and Ottis Sadler, and they started work on it in 1984 from plans "created in dreams and imaginations." Ickes, a reggae musician from Bermuda, wanted to express his devotion in some concrete form, and he conceived and designed the castle as an art project. Sadler was an illiterate tobacco field worker from North Carolina, and Ickes told him that if he put his heart and soul into the project, Ickes would name it after him. Scratching Ottis' name in the dirt, Ickes mistakenly spelled it with three *t*s. He looked at what he had written with wonder, seeing the *O* as the symbol of eternity, the *i* as the omnipresence of God, and the three *t*s as the three crosses on Calvary. In 1988 Ickes felt a "harmonic convergence, a sense of completeness." To him, the crenellations that topped the towers symbolized Jesus' crown of thorns. There were eighty-eight window openings, unglazed, unplanned, the same number as Harry Andrews's Ohio castle, the same as the number of keys on a piano; as a musician, Ickes held that to be significant. The interior of the castle remained unfinished. There were no utilities and no provision for them. Only the exterior had ever been visualized. As the castle was intended to be a sculpture, no thought had been given to an interior, but Father Robert Baker, the local parish priest, saw the possibilities and persuaded the men to complete it in the style of a tenth-century Irish church. The woodwork was done by a Tennessean appropriately named Lee Carpenter. This is serious stuff, but Ickes retains an awareness of the bizarre nature of his enterprise. "After work we'd sit under a bay tree and reflect on what we'd done that day, and we would burst out laughing at the enormity of it all." And he wasn't troubled by his lack of a building permit. One day shortly after the towers topped the trees and the structure became visible from the road, a building inspector friend of his came down the drive and said, "Rusty, what're you doing?" On hearing his response, another friend provided a permit for a garage, and that

A reggae musician and an illiterate tarheel built Castle Otttis, whose misspelled name is a miracle.

was that. Castle Otttis, an original sculpture done in remembrance of Jesus Christ, where more than thirty weddings have been held, including a Jewish ceremony, is officially a garage.

These last few dream castles have their air of unreality heightened by the lack of vast teams of laborers toiling unremittingly in the broiling sun to fulfill the insane megalomania of one man. With the arrival of the twentieth century came the realization that the most valuable resources are human life, spirit, imagination, and soul. Machines were invented to do the donkey work. Now ordinary people could build palaces, unconstrained by architects, engineers, surveyors, and dictators. They set to work with a will. They were also unconstrained by cheap labor so they had to do it all themselves, but that was no deterrent. It added to the pleasure. Joe Vallenino, building his house outside Watertown, Connecticut, confessed, "I don't want nobody working for me as it'd take away my incentative." Their castles, palaces, and dream houses were built with whatever material came to hand; sure, they would use marble and cut glass and Welsh slate and fine damask if it was lying around, but supplies of empty bottles, driftwood, printing plates, tin cans, scrap, and homemade concrete were more frequently available. Poured concrete was to architecture what desktop publishing was to typography. All of a sudden anybody could do it, and too many people did. Anyway, money is an irrelevance when you build castles.

But before we entirely leave this fantasy of palaces and castles, there is a final mysterious edifice to be glimpsed at a distance from the Versailles Road in Lexington, Kentucky. Behind a notice shouting KEEP OUT! WARRANTS WILL BE ISSUED AGAINST OWNERS AND/OR LICENSE NUMBERS OF TRESPASSING VEHICLES UNDER KRS 433. NO EXCEPTIONS! posted on a massive iron gate, in the bluegrass center of horse country, four long low walls join to make a huge castellated square, with octagonal towers capped by conical roofs at each corner. In the middle stands the castle keep, also low, with round turrets at each corner. The story goes that it was built by an adoring husband for his wife, who divorced him when she saw it. The truth is harder to unravel, but there are some known facts. The castle was conceived in Europe, when Caroline Bogaert Martin thought it would be nice to have a wall surrounding her home. Her husband Rex Martin, a real estate developer, purchased fifty-three acres of land along Versailles Road and Pisgah Pike. The plans for the castle were drawn up in 1968 and construction started the following year. The castle was still incomplete when the couple divorced in 1975. It was intended to have seven bedrooms, fifteen bathrooms, Italian fountains, and tennis courts; nothing was finished. It stands on a bare slope forlornly glowering at the highway like an aggressive recluse. There is always a police car parked in the driveway, but no cops are seen and speculation is that the police car, like the castle, is a sham. No work has been carried out on the site for years, and prominent For Sale notices are posted on the property. Call the number given, however, and a recorded message asks you to leave a number. You will never be called back. The privacy surrounding such a prominent building is remarkable. This was not something built by someone seeking privacy; it shouts its existence right across Woodford County. In 1988 it was valued by the local authorities at $554,000, an incomplete assessment because it was "still under construction." It is said that the asking price is currently an unrealistic $4 million. The castle bears an uncanny resemblance to the monastery of Sucevita in the Suceava province of Romania.

A massive gate and a sham police car guard a fifteen-bathroom palace on Versailles Road in Kentucky's bluegrass country.

ARCHITECTURAL FOLLIES IN AMERICA

Chapter 4

SCRAP
SHACKS

Paper, salt, coal, and bottles do not readily spring to mind as ideal building materials. Paper and salt seem particularly willful choices given their weathering properties; apart from the sheer difficulty of rendering the materials fit for construction, a fine air of unreality hangs over the whole enterprise. Why bother? What are they trying to prove? In the case of Elis Stenman the question nags away incessantly as fact after fact tumbles out about the history of his Paper House in Pigeon Cove, Massachusetts. From 1922 until the outbreak of war, toiling through the Great

The question nags: Why did Elis Stenman invest twenty years of his life in rolling up newspapers?

Depression, Stenman and his family rolled and folded newspapers, glueing, varnishing, and stapling, until they completed their dream: a house built entirely from paper. The outside walls, protected from the elements by a wide verandah, consist of two-inch-square lozenges of folded newspaper, further protected by coats of heavy clear varnish, browning with age, through which it is still possible to read enticing snatches of Boston life in the 1930s:

> were commented on admiringly . . .
> by radio experts here. The transmitting set . . .
> designed by the NBC . . .
> and extremely low . . .
> watt transmitter . . .
> one radio authority . . .
> side of an electric . . .
> park, found guilty . . .
> with a duck . . .

and the stories fade away into tantalizing tea-stained mystery as the side of the lozenge brutally cuts out sixty-year-old history. Not content with building the house from paper, Stenman furnished the interior completely out of paper. The curtains were made from the funnies, the only part of the papers to be printed in color at that time, and there is a paper radio dating from 1928. The house also contains a grandfather clock made from the daily newspapers from each of the capitals of the forty-eight continental states, and one desk constructed from copies of the *Christian Science Monitor* and another from newspapers reporting Lindbergh's solo flight across the Atlantic in 1927. The piano, the octagonal tables, chairs, and seats, even the fireplace (although the chimney, sensibly enough, is brick-built), all are made from tightly rolled newspapers that, we are informed, can theoretically still be unrolled and read. We were not allowed to verify this. And as we drive back down into the little coastal village of Pigeon Cove we are still baffled. Why did Elis Stenman feel it necessary to invest twenty years of his life rolling up newspapers? We are given an official answer: "This work was started merely as an experiment to see what could be done with newspapers without damaging the print. The experiment has proved a success both in strength and stability." Merely? Twenty years of merely experimenting? Well, now the world is wiser. Thank you, Mr. Stenman.

Salt is even sillier than paper as a building material. It dissolves in water almost as quickly as bourbon, so it needs to be sealed very carefully. Then again, perhaps it doesn't rain too much in Grand Saline, Texas, where the tiny Salt Palace, the world's only salt house, can be found. It was built in 1936, by C. O. Dixon, the manager of the Grand Saline Light and Power Company, to celebrate the Texas Centennial. Disappointingly it was never intended as a permanent home, but rather as a little museum to promote the general saltiness of the area. A new salt house was built to replace the old one, not quite as salty, as only two walls are covered, but the demise of the old building was sufficient to prove the uselessness of salt as a construction material. This is, unsurprisingly, unique. Nowhere else in the world did anyone bother to attempt building a house out of salt, although Lot's wife did have a brief but memorable career as a caryatid.

A house built out of coal? Check with your fire insurance company first, but if they demand a precedent you can point to Williamson, West Virginia, on the Kentucky border, where the chamber of commerce has housed itself comfortably on Second Avenue and Court Street in a single-story building whose walls are made from sixty-five tons of randomly cut bituminous coal, windows and doors arched with coal voussoirs. It was built in 1933 by H. T. Hicks and D. M. Goode, and externally it has maintained its integrity by being regularly coated with weatherproof varnish. You will have realized that Williamson is a coal mining community.

The peculiarly
American
phenomenon of
building houses
from bottles
seems to have
had its start in
Nevada.

ARCHITECTURAL FOLLIES IN AMERICA

Bottle houses appear to be a peculiarly American phenomenon; most of them seem to have been built out of necessity rather than whim, and the earliest examples are to be found in Nevada. The oldest bottle house in the state was William F. Peck's 1902 house in Tonopah, but it was torn down in the early 1980s. Two small bottle houses still struggle to survive in Goldfield, both on Main Street, the one at the edge of town now almost beyond repair due to the depredations of bottle hunters, the other, opposite the grimly castellated 1907 courthouse, still with most of its four walls standing. This was built with the bottles set diagonally in alternate courses. One brown rectangular bottle is molded "Patented 1902" on the bottom, so that allows us to postdate the house.

Ellen and Clint live in a five wheel (otherwise known as a mobile home) next to Tom Kelly's bottle house. Ellen and Clint are the only permanent inhabitants of Rhyolite, an entrancing ghost town in the Amargosa Desert. Rhyolite was founded in February 1905, after Frank "Shorty" Harris and Ernest L. Cross struck gold at their Bullfrog mine in the Bonanza Mountains. The town endured on stock speculation and wild surmise until the Montgomery-Shoshone mine closed in 1911. Right at the beginning of this frenzy Tom Kelly, a Welsh goldminer who came to Nevada by way of Australia, built himself a solid L-shaped house out of the only material more plentiful than gold in Rhyolite—beer bottles. He started work in September 1905, and 50,000 bottles later completed the

Tom Kelly built his house out of beer bottles— the only material more plentiful than gold in Rhyolite.

house in February 1906. Kelly used bottles because, as Ellen drily remarked, "It's very difficult to build a house with lumber from a Joshua tree." Rhyolite was the fastest boom and bust town ever; it went from nothing to a population of more than 10,000, with banks, churches, two railroads, a grand station, electric power and light, three water and sewage companies, a large concrete school for 250 pupils, hotels, restaurants, and a telephone exchange then back to nothing in an astonishing six years—SimCity made real. In 1920 the population was 14, by 1924 it was completely abandoned. The following year a location finder for Paramount Pictures discovered the deserted township and restored and reroofed the Bottle House for a movie, itself now lost. New tenants arrived; for a while it was run as a museum by Louis J. Murphy. In 1954 "Tommy" Thompson, who played the accordion in Rhyolite bars in 1905, moved in, created an extraordinary garden and raised eight children in the house, but even his fecundity could not revitalize Rhyolite. He died at the age of eighty in 1969, the last inhabitant of the Bottle House. Of this once booming city a few ruins remain: a couple of shacks, the ruins of the Cook Bank, the school, the railroad station in reasonable condition, and the sagging Bottle House. Thompson tried to repair it by putting concrete between the bottles instead of the adobe mud that Kelly had used and, because concrete has a different coefficient of expansion than adobe, the fierce desert heat has begun to crack some of the bottles. Something needs to be done urgently to preserve this historic monument. Anheuser-Busch, whose products were consumed in prodigious quantities to enable this house to be built, could easily make a gesture of support and fund its restoration. It would provide worldwide publicity for the company at very little cost.

In the 1930s Martin Lowman built himself a one-story house in a forest clearing between Ocala and Hernando, Florida, using one-gallon Clorox bleach bottles and a flint infill. Most of the bottles were clear, but he used brown bottles for framing and picking out geometrical patterns. He and his mother lived in this glass house with clear walls until 1979, when Ed Toi, a Texan trucker, bought the property. Ed has improved and expanded the house, although the roof has gone from the room nearest the road. There was a consistency and integrity about Lowman's work that Ed has maintained— Lowman was faithful to the Clorox brand and Ed has seen fit not to change, even getting in touch with the company, based on the West Coast, to try and get old bottles from them for repairs and replace-

ARCHITECTURAL FOLLIES IN AMERICA

ments. Unfortunately the one guy who was enthusiastic and promised to help has now left the company, and nobody else seems interested. To make matters worse, the highway department wants to convert the country road beside which the shack was originally built to a four-lane highway, obliterating the Bottle House in the process. America has many four-lane highways, but only a very few bottle houses. I heard that there was a house made out of 10,000 milk bottles in Tampa, Florida, but Lowman's Clorox Bottle House is probably it.

Martin Lowman knew the meaning of brand loyalty: all the thousands of bottles in his house once contained Clorox bleach.

Consistency and necessity were not uppermost in the mind of John Hope, pharmacist of Hillsville, Virginia, when he built his bottle house in 1940. Hope was the first man in town to have a swimming pool, and Miss Marshall, the Hillsville librarian, was lucky enough to be friendly with his daughter. In return Miss Marshall's mother, who worked in a restaurant, saved wine bottles and gave them to Doc Hope, who constructed a charming, polychromatic little house out of them, together with his used medicine bottles. This house was built for fun rather than necessity, and unlike all the other bottle houses, the bottles point outward so that the inner walls are flush and the little one-room summerhouse looks from the outside

like a technicolor hedgehog. The effect of the light inside the house
when the sun shines through the west wall is gorgeous, a stained
glass kaleidoscope, as if one were inside some secular temple.
Assuming the house to have been built largely of wine bottles dili-
gently emptied by Doc Hope, the townspeople christened his little
folly "The House of a Thousand Headaches."

The most ambitious bottle house in the nation became a bottle
village. It was started by an elderly lady—a rare example of a
woman driven by the compulsion to build and go on building, a
curiously male preserve. Grandma Prisbrey's Bottle Village stands
on a lot at 4595 Cochran Street, Simi Valley, California, a few miles
from Northridge, the epicenter of the January 1994 earthquake.
Grandma Penny, as her mailbox still describes her, started her Bottle Village in 1955 when she was sixty-two, and while she brought a
fresh sense of style and eccentricity to bottle building, incorporat-
ing automobile headlights, TV screens, car windshields, and fir

Grandma Prisbey began building her bottle-and-scrap masterpiece when she was sixty-two; she didn't stop until she'd created an entire village.

cones into her fantasies, she had no idea how to allow for earth-quakes. The quake has badly damaged her masterpiece, bringing down several walls and one entire and important building, the Pencil House. Several roofs appear to have collapsed, but it is difficult to check as the property has been sealed off with yellow police tape. The Pencil House was important because it was the start of the whole project. Grandma Prisbrey liked to collect things, and when her collection of 4,000 pencils grew too large for the trailer she lived in with her husband, she built the Pencil House out of bottles and other pieces of junk she picked up from the city dump, which she visited every day for more than twenty years. She also built a Leaning Tower of Pisa, a rumpus room, a shell house, a doll house, the Little Chapel, a cabana, Cleopatra's Bedroom, and more, using over a million bottles. The state and fate of Grandma Prisbrey's Bottle Village is uncertain. One hopes that funds will be available for its restoration now that it has been designated a California Historical Monument as well as a Ventura County Cultural Landmark. A nonprofit organization, Preserve Bottle Village, has been set up to repair and restore it.

Charlie Yelton began building his bottle houses in Forest City, North Carolina, in 1971. Charlie had seen a television program about a bottle house out West (Rhyolite? Grandma Prisbrey?) and reckoned he could do that, too. He had just retired after working for the Florence Mill for fifty years, and needed something to occupy himself. Four years and 11,987 bottles later Charlie had three bottle houses, a glass wishing well, and a glass flower garden all built out of beer and whiskey bottles, as well as 7-Up and Milk of Magnesia bottles. Nor had he any idea of how to build a house. "I just started building and laid it out as I went," he explained. As with Doc Hope's bottle house in Virginia, there is an ecclesiastical gleam to the interior, a secular stained glass effect that gave Charlie peace: "I come here pretty often when I feel I want to be alone with the Lord. I just kneel down here and talk to the Lord for a while. When I leave here I feel a lot better." Charlie Yelton died in 1993, and as with Grandma Prisbrey, the future of his rare work is undecided.

There is another bottle house in Yettem, California, and a newish one built by Knott's Berry Farm for their sham ghost town in Calico, California. There was a very fine example in Pittman, Nevada, called the House of Lost Memories, or Parker's Castle. Not only has it been demolished but Pittman itself has disappeared from Clark County on the official state map. There are also some fine bottle houses in Canada. Bottle houses are uniquely North American architectural manifestations, and more care should be taken to preserve them.

Scrap shacks do not have mighty porticos, Palladian windows, or cupolas, except those thrown up by Lurelle Guild in Darien, Connecticut. Guild, a noted industrial designer whose work has been exhibited at the Museum of Modern Art and the Brooklyn Museum, had a penchant for making houses happen. He would scout architectural salvage yards, demolition contractors, and junk shops for anything that caught his fancy. He would then reerect the parts with a blithe disregard for form, convention, or classical rules. A reerected barn looked too plain to him, so he added a Georgian doorway with pilasters. Ordinary frame houses acquired architectural accretions until their visual coherence gratefully collapsed under the weight of conflicting motifs. They became scrap palaces rather than scrap shacks, miniature Biltmores and Versailles, and some of them carried names of equal grandeur such as Boscobel and Monticello. Guild was interested only in construction, not maintenance. His houses began the irreversible process of decay the moment building ceased; he wanted nothing further to do with them. Three of them were torn down within two years of his death in 1985. A few survive. Guild's philosophy was encapsulated in the title of an article he wrote in 1943 for *House and Garden:* "The House Just Happened." As all the best buildings do, of course. In the same state of mind William Dudley built a house at Fishkill, New York, in 1854. It was described as "an architectural curiosity of the first water, built from pieces of various Greek Revival structures by a demolition contractor." The doorsill came from the cage of Samson The Bear, a famous New York attraction in the mid-nineteenth century.

Interstate highway 80 through northern Nevada, enthusiastically dubbed the "Wagon Master Trail" by the state's tourism commission, is a worthy contender for the dullest road in America. Dull it most certainly is, all the way through the high desert to Imlay when suddenly one of the most remarkable structures in the West leaps into view. This is Thunder Mountain, not a mountain at all, but a folly house and garden built by Chief Rolling Mountain Thunder, who was not Chief Rolling Mountain Thunder at all. If that seems confusing, there is worse to come. Thunder Mountain is or was a house, unlike any other house anywhere. Its nearest relative must be the Watts Towers, simply because they share cement and bottles and broken tiles in their construction. It is hard to figure out the shape of the house; better to say it could once have looked like an enormous shopping basket but now it defies methodical description. Listing some of the materials used in its construction may begin to indicate its eclecticism—typewriters, concrete, stones, bottles, television screens, cans, ceramic insulators, tiles, car windshields, slate, skulls, cement—you get the picture. Sometimes there is almost a hint of normality: it is possible to discern on the third story a standard pitched roof, but it is so swamped by the riot of cement statues and swathed by concrete ropes, all daubed in every available color of paint, that the eye simply ignores it as being out of place. There is one large ground floor topped with a concrete tree of life and two smaller upper stories, contained within a 47-foot-high arch made out of metal rods covered with cement. Spears pierce the arch. Around the house are placed farm implements, giant concrete statues (among them Sitting Bull and Sarah Winnemucca), old pick-up trucks, a crane, a forge, a couple of peacocks, and too much else to note. Further description is futile; only a visit can do this fantastic place justice, together with some background information.

It was begun in 1968, as a "Monument to the First Inhabitants of the West, the American Indians, by Chief Rolling Mountain Thunder," says the information board at the deserted entrance. And we learn that Chief Rolling Mountain Thunder was born Frank van Zant in Oklahoma on the eleventh day of the eleventh month of the eleventh year of the twentieth century. He had a varied life, much of it rootless and wandering: deputy sheriff, airman in World War II,

The walls of Chief Rolling Mountain Thunder's remarkable house are covered with homilies and out-and-out ravings.

Methodist minister, logger, police officer, miner, archeology student at Berkeley, private detective. A quarter Cree Indian, he was passionate about his spiritual heritage and, unable to articulate his passions, he turned to construction as a means of expression, as we have seen before. Texts, homilies, and straightforward ravings cover the grounds and the walls of the erection, generally taking an antifederal government stance and defending Indian tribes. Chief Rolling Mountain Thunder was interviewed as his work progressed. "My purpose is to add something worthwhile to America. It will never be completed as long as I am alive. When I die, only then will it be done." He committed suicide on the site on January 8, 1989.

If an old railroad car sounds like a good home for a hobo, an old Pullman coach should be home to the King of the Road. In Medora, North Dakota, someone expressed himself by covering an entire Pullman with cobblestones for his own mysterious ends. And from a Pullman coach to Pullman, Washington, where Vic Moore, who

Chief Rolling Mountain Thunder—no chief, but one-quarter Cree Indian—wanted "to add something worthwhile to America."

lectures at Washington State University, lives in his thesis. The Moorage, Moore's scrap shack, was built as part of his thesis for a master's degree in fine arts, and he described it as "a big asssemblage which has absolutely no practical, utilitarian function like architecture." Nevertheless it has a crazy cohesion, two turrets with finials mimicking a conventional Victorian bay window, but created from corrugated iron rather than granite.

Houston's apparent lack of zoning laws have allowed for a splendid variety of eccentricities within the city. On Malone Street near Memorial Park a house covered in flattened beer cans can scarcely be seen for the shimmering, clicking curtains of pull tabs and can tops and bottoms that drape the entire structure. The Beer Can House was a plain frame dwelling until John Milkovisch retired and decided to do something with the cans he hadn't recycled. Again we meet a busy, practical man with time on his hands. This one liked beer, a lot. The bottle-house builders all denied sampling the product; Milkovisch happily put away 50,000 cans of the amber nectar before he started to flatten them to provide himself with free siding. He added the tab curtains, ostensibly to help reduce air conditioning costs, then went on to add arches in the garden, a ladder to the sky, and fences sparkling with marbles until he died in 1988. Son Ronnie is carrying on the tradition, and he has built a solid beer can fence and gate in front of the house.

Nearby on Floyd Street is Tempietto Zeni, an architect-designed house, but one that needed an extremely idiosyncratic client—in this case the architect himself, Frank Zeni. Three mighty, asymmetrical Ionic columns made out of corrugated steel provide the initial shock of Zeni's house. He has reinterpreted the classical orders in commonly available material, and the end product, although bizarre to behold, works.

Another temple, on Munger Street this time, is dedicated to the orange. As far as Jeff McKissack, the retired postal worker who started the Orange Show, was concerned, oranges were the only fruit. The Orange Show, which took him twenty years to construct after he retired in 1959, is a paean of praise to the orange; it is quite literally a temple. There are tracts on How You Can Live 100 Years And Still Be Spry (the answer involves oranges), mottoes, posters, and exhortations. Architecturally the structure can barely be made out underneath the weight of orangephenalia, flags, masts, wheels, and colored wrought iron. McKissack was seriously impressed by oranges. The Orange Show is now a major cultural center in Houston.

Joseph Vallenino has had a hard life. He was brought up poor. He bought a little old house on the side of the Nonewaug River on Route 6 in Woodbury, Connecticut, back in 1972 when he was forty, and started to build on it in 1975. Twelve years later his brother died. Vallenino said it broke him up, so he worked the grief out of his system by engulfing the little old house in a great mansion. A low-pitched roof covers the entire structure, rising to four stories. The house is now L-shaped with tiers of classical columns at the base of the L. He has built every bit of the mansion himself. "How do I find the time? I don't hang out in gin mills, that's how. Look at these columns. Know how much they cost?" Joe, working as a demolition contractor, acquired the cast-iron columns at some unbelievably low price from a warehouse he was taking down in Bridgeport. The extension is roofed with the best quality Vermont slate. Gray, green, and purple Vermont slate tiles cost $2.50 a piece, but the red slates are $7.50 each. And red they are—not another shade of mauve or lilac, but a good strong terra-cotta red. Joe uses them for highlight and emphasis. He never uses scrap in the construction, only high-quality materials that may have been previously used. It doesn't diminish the quality. Joe's mansion is his life. It doesn't really matter if he never finishes it; he's happy just to work on it and talk about it.

Joe Vallenino found the time to build a mansion by not hanging out in gin mills.

Real scrap was used in the construction of a deliberately eccentric residence in the elegant Welsh village of Cambria on California's beautiful central coast. Art Beal was a character; blessed with a nose like an exploding eggplant, he liked to call himself "Captain Nitwit" or "Der Tinkerpaw," while his less tolerant neighbors knew him as "The Fool on the Hill." Beal had the colorful background usually only granted to first novelists, working as a dishwasher and vaudeville comedian, losing his mother (a Klamath Indian, of course) in the 1906 San Francisco earthquake, becoming a champion swimmer with Johnny Weissmuller, working with Dr. Linus Pauling, even touring with Willie Nelson, but his house is what made him famous. It began in 1928 when he was thirty-two, as a one-room shack on an awkward site—well, a cliff face—on Hillcrest Drive. Over the years it grew relentlessly, upward and outward, improved with beer cans, bottles, televisions, hub caps, river rock, abalone shells, paint cans, toilet seats, radios, old tin signs, window frames, salvaged doors, anything the captain could lay his hands on. "I had no more in mind of doing this than growing feathers," he remarked, but there it stands, precariously embracing the hillside in and on nine levels, designated a California Registered Historical Landmark in 1981, while he was still alive, and rapidly falling into decay and disrepair now that he is dead.

Near Pueblo, Colorado, a cluster of scruffy Buckminster Fuller-inspired geodesic domes mushroomed in 1965, acquiring the name Drop City after the dropouts who built them. They were constructed from scrap metal such as car roofs, painted in Detroit's original selection of colors but otherwise undecorated, the opposite of individuality (which is not a desirable trait in communal life). In the 1970s Mike Nichols in Taos, New Mexico, also chose the scrap route for his dwelling but preferred to call it recycled, which has a more ecologically correct air. He used bottles, tires, aluminum cans, and old lumber in his construction, but the most interesting features were the walls, which were made of old tires laid in a Flemish Bond pattern and then plastered. This makes a great deal of sense; you end up with 20-inch-thick walls with excellent insulation in winter and summer, at very low cost. They probably bounce around in earthquakes quite well, too.

The eeriest house in America is not the Bates mansion from Hitchcock's *Psycho*, but a simple, unassuming little house standing in a quiet suburb of Petersburg, Virginia. Near the junction of Youngs Road and Squall Level Road, an area of modest houses with fair-sized yards, stands this one exception, a silent, stone house, empty and

The eeriest house in America is not the Bates mansion—it's this sensible-looking house in Petersburg, Virginia.

neglected. It sits square and sensible on its lot, two stories, three windows at the front, two windows at the side, and a thousand widows within. For this house was not built of ordinary stone. To stand apart from its wooden neighbors, it was built of solid marble, the marble of nearly 2,000 tombstones of Union soldiers killed in the siege of Petersburg. The town is not particularly proud of its gruesome domicile; it is way off the tourist track and few townsfolk are even aware of its existence. The curator of the Petersburg Museum explained that what appears to have happened is that, to save on maintenance, all the tombstones were removed from Poplar Grove cemetery and sold to a Mr. O. E. Young, the builder of this house. No one in the town particularly wanted to spend money maintaining Union graves, so the sale reduced costs considerably. Some people may have thought this was justice, as 60,000 people were killed in the siege of Petersburg, which lasted for ten months until April 1865. The only visitors the house now gets are people looking for the gravestones of their ancestors. The tombstones face inward, so as the owner lay in bed the names of the dead stood about his head; later they were plastered over so that their descendants leave none the wiser. Because of the mild dereliction of the house—it is slowly being restored by a gentleman from North Carolina—one of the markers has become visible: carved in relief out of a Union shield is the name of 4754 August Hatinar, from New York. The last word must be left to the lady living next door to the Tombstone House, who confessed with massive political incorrectness, "Ah don't rightly see what all the fuss was about. They was jist Union boys."

Chapter 5

MIRACLE HOUSES (THE AMERICAN DREAM)

G reat idealists stand serene and certain among their uncomfortable contemporaries who will, in the main, resort to mockery. It was ever so; the object of ridicule smiles quietly and murmurs, "Time will prove me right." When no limits are set, this can never be denied.

Hexagons, octagons, decagons, dodecahedrons, circles—American builders of the nineteenth and twentieth centuries embraced the concept of living in the round more enthusiastically than had their European or Asiatic forebears. Sub-Saharan huts and Native American teepees seem to have had a greater influence on the individualistic home builder than any number of castellations or drawbridges. In Europe round buildings were largely ceremonial: the Pantheon in Rome, the church of San Vitale in Ravenna, the Choragic Monument of Lysicrates in Athens. Or they were meant to be jocular: the Colonne Détruite at the Désert de Retz in France. In Britain, the monopteros, the rotunda temple, became a favorite garden ornament, while whitewashed round houses in Veryan, Cornwall, were said to have been built to confuse the devil. Two ladies built a sixteen-sided house called A La Ronde in Devon in 1798, unique in Britain, but America pulled effortlessly ahead with many good examples of the genre.

A magnificent sixteen-sided barn in Hayfield, Virginia, dating from 1886, was burned down in 1967. Buckminster Fuller's geodesic dome was enthusiastically embraced by alternative thinkers, a

This dispirited golf ball sits on a tee in the drab Arizona desert outside Yucca.

fatal accolade resulting in an ill-lit and gloomy 128-sided globe perched on a service shaft in the drab Arizona desert outside Yucca; a dispirited golf ball on a tee in an infinite bunker. Even the mail box, a half-hearted replica of its parent, fails to raise a smile. The essential flaw is that the original design cannot be expanded, and the necessary accumulations of everyday life like the discarded refrigerator and the pick-up with the flat tires huddle mournfully about the base with no real home to go to.

In 1960 Clay Lancaster published an enjoyably idiosyncratic book entitled *The Architectural Follies of America,* which I had hoped to plagiarize extensively until I discovered that much of what he described had been torn down years before he described it. However, Lancaster kindled my enthusiasm for a favorite style of his: the octagon house. Initially unconvinced, I became an unquestioning believer after seeing the Armour-Stiner House in Irvington-on-Hudson, New York, and reading Orson Squire Fowler's seminal work *A Home For All.* Fowler was a successful phrenologist and publisher, but above all he was a promoter and popularizer. He spent the first part of his working life as a phrenologist, a now-discredited science that has been replaced by psychology, and, like modern psychologists, much of his work was concerned with sex, health, and the family. He attributed much of the world's misery, unhappiness, and ill health to inadequate living conditions, and resolved to revolutionize them.

Convenience was a major concern. "An unhandy house . . . by perpetually irritating mothers, sours the tempers of their children, even *before birth*, thus rendering the whole family bad-dispositioned *by nature*." This led him, by a leap of deduction not easy to comprehend, to recommend the octagon as the ideal format for a residence. There is not space here to recount the myriad ways that Fowler convinced himself and many others of the superiority of the octagon over any ordinary building, but his persuasiveness can be gauged from the fact that more than 1,000 octagonal houses were built in America in the twenty years following the publication of *A Home For All*. There are some octagonal houses elsewhere in the world, but nothing like America's treasure trove.

Fowler's passion was for concrete. The original 1848 title of his book was *A Home For All or a New, Cheap, Convenient, and Superior Mode of Building*. The 1853 edition was retitled *A Home For All or The Gravel Wall and Octagon Mode of Building New, Cheap, Convenient, Superior and Adapted to Rich and Poor*. The "gravel wall" was, of course, concrete. Fowler's mentor in this area was Joseph Goodrich of Milton, Wisconsin. Fowler had visited him in 1850 and had been hugely impressed by the concrete buildings Goodrich had erected, as well as by his showmanship—he gave Fowler a sledgehammer and told him to hit the inside of his parlor wall "as hard as I pleased" for six cents per blow, which he said would repair all damages. Fowler was distressed by the reaction of the locals to Goodrich's first experiments in concrete. "He first built an academy not larger than a school-house. Part way up, a severe storm washed it, so that a portion fell. His neighbors wrote on it with chalk by night, 'Goodrich's folly.' But after it was up, he wrote in answer, 'Goodrich's wisdom.'"

Fowler practiced what he preached. Between Fishkill and Wappinger's Falls in New York State he began to build, in 1847, a mammoth three-story octagon house, which inevitably became known as Fowler's Folly. Due to lack of funds it took nearly ten years to construct; despite the financial and critical success of *A Home For All* and the author's claims for the cheapness of his methods, a 65-room house will always be expensive to build. He had already warned his readers not to "endanger bankruptcy, or spend beyond your means" but for Fowler the cost was incidental, as he wrote: "No labor of my life has given me more lively delight than the planning and building of my house." The truth of this is apparent in the subsequent history of the house. One obvious flaw in the octagon design is that it cannot be extended without compromising its integrity; when the house is finished it is finished, and there is an end to it. It can only be extended vertically. The house was finally completed in 1857, and almost immediately Fowler leased it to a William A. Riker for five years. The only reasonable explanation for Fowler's action, apart from a cash-flow crisis, is that having completed his house he lost interest and found something else to do. Time after time this behavior is seen in folly builders. They either work on their buildings forever, completing them only in death, or they actually finish the project, in which case they lose interest and move away. Chief Rolling Mountain Thunder is an example of the first type; Simon Rodia and Orson Squire Fowler the second. Unfortunately, Fowler's theories, like his gravel walls, were not impermeable. Riker used the huge structure as a boarding house, and the following summer a typhoid epidemic broke out in it. Sewage had seeped through Fowler's "impermeable" coarse concrete walls, decimating the lodgers. A new tenant, Professor Cassard, ran a military school for young Spaniards in the house but decamped without paying the rent. Fowler's Folly was then rented by a Mrs. Berdell as a guest house, but the inhabitants of Fishkill decided that the poor woman was a notorious mass murderess of the same name. This did not encourage potential guests, and by the time the real murdering Mrs. Berdell had been apprehended, the business had collapsed. The house limped on with a succession of tenants, progressively shabbier. Repairs were made in 1880 but Fowler died in 1887, and the house fell into ruin. In August, 1897, the structure was dynamited "because of the danger to visitors who still come to see Fowler's Folly." The local newspaper, the *Fishkill Standard*, reported at the time that "it used to be bought or sold on the New York Stock Exchange when the members had no more exciting occupation."

Despite this catalog of failures, a magnificent vindication of Fowler's theories survives in splendid condition at Irvington-on-Hudson, a few miles from Fishkill. Built by Philip Armour in 1860, it was adored by a subsequent owner, Philip Stiner, who enlarged it by adding a huge multicolored dome in purple, blue, and red slate, and further decked out the house with an encircling veranda, a cupola, wildly elaborate bargeboards, and all the appurtenances that befit a gentleman's residence, including a ballroom. Memorably described as "an arrested carousel," it remains one of the most unusual and distinctive private houses in America. Over the past fifteen years it has been sensitively and carefully restored to its full polychromatic plum pudding glory by an architect and artist, Mr. and Mrs. Joseph Pelli.

The Armour-Stiner House is a magnificent vindication of a phrenologist's theories about the benefits of octagonal living.

After the Armour-Stiner House the most astonishing octagon house in the nation is Nutt's Folly, or Longwood, south of Natchez, Mississippi. It is a vast mansion, the octagon form being disguised by the addition of rectangular rooms on every other facet. The whole gigantic edifice is topped with an onion dome. Samuel Sloan promoted this exotic Oriental design in his two-volume work, *The Model Architect*, published in Philadelphia in 1852. Dr. Haller Nutt, recently returned from successfully smuggling cotton seeds out of Egypt, saw the book and found his dream home. He commissioned Sloan to design the house and construction started in 1861, rather unfortunately for Dr. Nutt, who was a Union sympathizer. It is said that he flew the American flag over his unfinished house at this most inappropriate time, so Confederate troops burned his cotton fields. Distressed, he hauled up the Confederate flag just as the Union troops arrived, so they in turn burned his ginmill, sawmill, and three further plantations. Nutt gave up and left. Longwood has more justification for the title of folly than the Armour-Stiner house, as construction was then halted before the house was finished, and it has remained uncompleted since then. Despite these rumors and legends, members of the Nutt family held onto the house, living in the basement until the 1960s. Now it is a museum owned by the Pilgrimage Garden Club; the internal scaffolding is still erect and the workmen's tools are still on site, waiting for Dr. Nutt to return and complete the job, just as they have been for more than a century.

Several octagon homes still stand, along with a very few that pre-date Fowler's epiphany. Lack of time has prevented a pilgrimage to the sites of all the known survivors, but this totally American passion needs to be preserved. Perhaps an Octagon Society? Members could drive around in octagonally badged MGs, now almost as rare.

While there is nothing in America to compare with the Chevalier de Monville's hugely eccentric concentric house outside Paris in the form of a ruined column, mentioned earlier—which so caught the imagination of Thomas Jefferson that both the Capitol and Monticello show traces of Monville's influence—there are some examples of earlier octagons and circles. Monticello, the house many Americans regard as their ideal home, is octagonal, as is Jefferson's 792-acre retreat at Poplar Forest in Lynchburg, Virginia, which has a small octagonal house that burned down in the mid-nineteenth century and has since been rebuilt. At the time of visiting, in 1993, it was again under repair, with the foundations being underpinned.

It is symmetrically flanked by two brick-built octagonal outhouses, tactfully described by Jefferson's mason: "I have finished one Necessary," he wrote in 1811, "I shall finish the other next week." Fowler never refers to Jefferson's unusual passion for the octagon mode, which seems a strange omission.

Thomas Jefferson's octagonal house at his Poplar Forest retreat is flanked by twin octagonal "necessaries."

Col. John Tayloe III commissioned Dr. William Thornton, the primary architect of the Capitol, to design for him a family house in Washington, D.C., known as The Octagon, which was completed in 1802. Although the structure still stands, surrounded by the head-quarters for the American Institute of Architects, it seems to have inspired but one imitator, a house on the corner of Sixteenth and U Streets, N.W. This may be due to the fact that no part of The Octagon is remotely octagonal. It was built on a 70-degree-angled corner lot, an inevitable concomitant of a radial city centrally planned, and Thornton's solution was pragmatic and elegant: two main reception rooms angled to the shape of the lot, abutting a circular hall with a further circular stairwell, and an oval room and service rooms linking the two main wings. Not an octagon in sight. It is built of a lovely salmon-pink brick with fine white mortaring, but there is little of the folly about it aside from the cost. Originally estimated at $13,000 in 1799, the construction bill alone (before fitting out) came in a year later at $35,000. Washington defense contractors must have learned a lot from this early example.

Not until 1829 do we find a surviving circular home, but this one was described to me as truly bizarre: a figure eight rather than an octagon, and apparently nicknamed the Jew's Harp House for its passing resemblance in plan to that melodic instrument. The reality is less fanciful. Seth Strong's spectacular attempt at family housing in Northampton, Massachusetts, caused all the rumors to fly but in fact there is no figure eight, no octagon, and no Jew's Harp to be seen— it is simply a large round brick-built house with a conical roof. At the rear is the one-story rectangular ell which may have given rise to the house's old nomenclature, now only half remembered. It is the earliest surviving round house in New England, but again it had few imitators. Fifteen years later, in Middletown, Rhode Island, two shipbuilding brothers built themselves a now-demolished circular house, while the distinguished architect Charles Follen McKim, of McKim, Mead and White, designed a surviving shingled round house in the 1890s for Daniel S. Newhall in Jamestown, Rhode Island, on Conanicut, a hideaway now bridged to the outside world. "No gorgeous palaces uprear / Their walls of pomp and folly here," wrote Henry S. Frieze about Conanicut in 1844.

In Texarkana, Texas, James H. Draughn extended the octagon theory by building three of them together, then adding a porch at the bottom. Voilà: the Ace of Clubs. Draughn, of Welsh ancestry, was born in Tennessee in 1843, the son of an innkeeper. He worked in California, Nevada, Kentucky, Ohio, and Tennessee before arriving in Texarkana in 1873, where he worked in dry goods and lumber. Here he began to make serious money, and he founded the First National Bank of Texarkana. Such an elevated position required a house of similar eminence, and in 1883 he constructed this late flowering of the octagon style in brick, stuccoed and scored to resemble stone. Sadly, the unknown architect's ingeniously designed floor plan gave rise to stories that Draughn had financed the building of the house by winning a fortune at cards, not the most illustrious pedigree for a would-be respected banker. Perhaps this was the reason that lay behind his decision within three years to sell his house to W. L. Whitaker and move to Sulphur Station. The house later belonged to the Moore family who lived in it for ninety-one years until it was bequeathed to the Texarkana Historical Society in 1985. Orson Squire Fowler's inspiration came not from common observation but from genuine originality of thought. Before Fowler, houses in this format were rare. After the publication of his book, they proliferated.

Throughout this book we have seen examples of mild eccentricity, megalomania, pride, passion, and futility, all best expressed in architecture. Each of these edifices has a little touch of individuality that allows us to grace them with the title of folly. But nothing can ever deserve that title quite so much as Sarah L. Winchester's house in San Jose, California, a folly to define follies. The Winchester Mystery House, a mansion now surrounded by suburbia, is the finest folly house in America, and nowhere in its extensive documentation or its gift shop the size of Macy's is there a mention of the word folly. Sarah Winchester's fortune came, together with her guilt, from the Winchester Rifle Company. In 1884, she lost her only child, and shortly afterwards, her husband (who left her $20 million), and she became convinced that her bad luck came from the spirits of the thousands who had been killed by Winchester repeaters, particularly the Indians. She escaped from chilly Connecticut to the warm, fertile farmlands of San Jose and bought a modest farmhouse called Llanda Villa. Few people are as gullible as the very rich, and Sarah Winchester had been told that in order to placate the spirits of the dead, she would have to build incessantly. She did. From 1884 until the day she died in September, 1922, construction on her house

Sarah Winchester tried to assuage her guilt by building incessantly—for thirty-eight years.

never stopped—24 hours a day, 7 days a week, 365 days a year. She was not too overcome by remorse to refuse the $1,000-a-day royalties that the guns brought her. Her grief and fear were introspective, as seen throughout this three-dimensional maze. The house is turned in upon itself, with stairs leading to ceilings, windows opening into other rooms, doors with blank walls behind them, and steps going down to go up. The owners, who have turned the house into a major tourist attraction, play up the mystery by leading tour parties on a tortuous trail a mile long through the house, constantly changing levels and aspects, now up, now down, now out, now in, warning tourists not to stray from the party for fear of getting lost. Near the middle of the house is the so-called Séance Room, a plain room like every other, with one entrance and three exits. We are told that Mrs. Winchester used this room not just for séances but for keeping an eye on her servants in the kitchen below—an internal window overlooks a light well above the kitchen. It is easy to conjure her up as a malevolent presence beating heavily in the heart of the house but there is no malevolence here, only fear and anxiety and insecurity, an elaborate series of defenses against an imagined foe.

The present owners lead tour parties on a tortuous, mile-long maze through the Winchester Mystery House.

ARCHITECTURAL FOLLIES IN AMERICA

Perhaps the most surprising thing about all these follies is the lack of a real ghost story attached to any of them. The buildings must have enough character without the need for the spiritual dimension. Sarah Winchester hammered and sawed her way to tranquillity, but it was a prophylactic measure, no record existing of a haunting at the house apart from a short catalog (which mysteriously ends in 1982) of the "eerie" experiences of Winchester Mystery House guides, impartially compiled by the press office. Not even the Tombstone House in Petersburg, Virginia, has inspired a good haunt, but another Petersburg resident was as wary of the unknown as Mrs. Winchester. This was Charles O'Hara, who built his Trapezium House on North Market Street in 1815, following the advice of his much admired West Indian servant, who warned him that as evil spirits loved right-angled corners they should be avoided at all costs. O'Hara built his house accordingly. Face on, it is an elegant three-story Georgian brick town house, a valuable piece of real estate if it didn't confront a junkyard for distressed Jaguars. Move a little way to either side, however, and the construction ceases to make any sense. Each side wall angles back at about 60 degrees, so you can look at a flat façade from virtually anywhere in front of the house. The house was not O'Hara's only oddity. He was a staunch Irish monarchist, and paraded through the city in full British Army regalia every Saint Patrick's Day. Do not condemn him; at that time Ireland was part of the United Kingdom.

Every decade throws up its House of the Future, and every decade we carry on living in the same old houses and apartments that we have lived in for centuries. Apart from modern insulation and the provision of utilities, there is little conceptual difference between a house built today and one erected by the Pilgrim fathers. Some past houses of the future survive, however, still valiantly struggling against the tides of fashion, exotic archaisms in a bland, homogenized world. Be it to pioneer the use of a new material, to demonstrate a theory, to prove an alternative method of construction, or to reduce costs, much of mankind's wilder creativity and ingenuity has been put into attempts to improve his living quarters. Not all of it has been equally effective. I am still working, without any lively hope of success, on a machine that tidies up after me. Domestic improvements have come gradually, not in sudden spurts; your average everyday house of the future holds too many new ideas to be assimilated with ease. But dream homes usually have one or two novelties that make it into common life.

MIRACLE HOUSES (THE AMERICAN DREAM)

In Beverly Shores, Indiana, a twelve-sided, glass-walled house started life in 1933, billed as the "House of Tomorrow" in the Century of Progress International Exhibition in Chicago. It was designed by George Fred Keck, who was distantly inspired by none other than Orson Squire Fowler. Before building the House of Tomorrow he made a detailed study of the Richards House in Watertown, Wisconsin, one of the largest octagon houses built. "I have the first dishwasher ever made," now boasts the owner of the House of Tomorrow. Of course it doesn't work, but who cares? This demonstrates the interdependency of progress. Industrial dishwashers had first appeared in the mid-nineteenth century, but the invention of Calgon in 1932 allowed the House of the Future to incorporate a domestic dishwasher only a year later. From such improvements our life is made; plumbing, electricity, central heating, air conditioning, all interconnected, one step at a time.

The Metropolitan Museum of Modern Art commissioned an aluminum house as a high-tech experiment in the 1930s. It has been put up and taken down several times in its life, and is currently living on the campus at the New York Institute of Technology. But how many of us now live in aluminum houses (excluding trailers and siding)? The giant steps for mankind attempted by our dream builders are necessary to keep us moving forward; it doesn't matter that they sometimes fall short or trip over their enthusiasms.

Thomas Edison took a break from his phonographs and light bulbs to devise a means of pouring concrete into house-sized molds. This allowed for the factory prefabrication of houses, dramatically reducing costs and, with remarkable prescience, saving trees. The best known surviving example was built in 1912 in Upper Montclair, New Jersey, near Edison's own home. It is surprisingly elegant for a house built out of concrete, complete with classical pilasters and parapet. One associates prefabricated concrete molds with low-rent housing, but this was evidently carefully and thoughtfully designed. "It has never leaked," says the owner proudly. Why didn't the idea catch on? Because house-sized molds are not the most wieldy constructions, and although the method reduced costs on the basis of long production runs, the start-up cost proved prohibitive.

Pouring a fine concrete silt *in situ* is one of the important processes at Arcosanti, Paolo Soleri's vast concept in central Arizona. Arcosanti is intended to be a near self-sufficient community of about 5,000 people, a city independent yet part of its environment. Work has been going on for twenty-five years, carried out by disciples of Soleri who pay for the privilege to work there. The project—which we are assured is finite—is about 3 percent complete. This means that at the present rate of progress the work should be complete by the year 2827, by which time its concept may look dated. But the theory behind Arcosanti and its smaller sibling, Cosanti in Scottsdale, is not architecture but *arcology*, a word coined by Soleri. Arcology, says Soleri, is the concept of architecture and ecology working as one integral process to produce new urban habitats. Its motif, the architectural form that has impassioned him, is the apse. The apse, till now almost exclusively used in ecclesiastical architecture, makes its appearance in various sizes and guises throughout the scheme. It was originally a purely functional design, intended to amplify and reflect sound from priest to congregation, but the reasons for its use in the context of Arcosanti remain unclear. The development is neither heated nor air conditioned; perhaps electronic amplification is frowned upon and apses are used as natural loudspeakers. The population of the complex in 1994 stood at about 70, plus a pride of friendly, contented cats. Critical mass—the stage when the builders will cease to pay for their work and the completion time of the project will be dramatically shortened—is slated to happen when the population exceeds 500. This is not a folly. It is a brave, exciting, and hugely ambitious project. Unfortunately it is also ugly. Should it be abandoned, or fail to be completed, or if Soleri's theories prove unworkable, then it will become a folly.

Poured concrete is yesterday's material, according to Roy Mason, the architect of Xanadu, the "Home of the Future" in Kissimmee, Florida. "Cross the time threshold of Xanadu, and experience 2001 technology today!" shouts a brochure. Xanadu is a conglomeration of blobs built in 1983 to demonstrate how houses could be built quickly and cheaply by spraying plastic balloons with polyurethane foam. It took forty days and the cost was $900,000. With the fervor of the true believer or a Fowler, Mason proclaims that more than one thousand private homes have now been built using this method, that it is bugproof and virtually fireproof, that it cannot rot (so bits of Xanadu will be with us throughout eternity), that it is wind resistant and energy efficient. He cannot understand why we are not all living in our own private Xanadus. Maybe he's right. From past performances it is a fair bet that at least one idea from Xanadu will be part of everyday life in a hundred years' time. Bugproof would be good.

Chapter 6

PARKS AND GARDENS

$\mathcal{F}$olly gardens and parks are lots of fun. Until now we have looked at the folly to be found in architecture, but that is only one aspect of the made environment. We shape our landscapes to our whims or purposes, and the individuality that shines out from folly shacks and palaces will find expression in even freer forms in parks and gardens. Classical European gardens abounded with allusion and imagery, objects to recall distant lands, buildings to emphasize human folly and frailty. The common inheritance, arrived at independently by creative souls, is for a garden to tell a story. Everyone has a story to tell. Why should it be any odder to tell it in poured concrete rather than in words or music? This desire, this means of self-expression, is a worldwide phenomenon, investigated pictorially by the Frenchman Bernard Lassus in his pioneering book *Jardins Imaginaires*, "Dream Gardens." America has its dream gardens, its parks of passions, where one thought, one obsession drives the builder (often a man of advancing years) to throw up structures as regularly and randomly as a dog scratches for fleas. The irritation of obsession will never be satisfied; few of these parks were or will be completed. As in the Winchester House, the very act of construction is the life force. When building stops, the glory departs. We are left with the coral reef, multicolored and perhaps beautiful to behold, but the heart is dead. It is then that these unique and extraordinary creations are most at risk. Then they can be torn down or redeveloped. Some few survive, acquiring local fame, becoming low-key tourist attractions for level-five visitors. (Level One: Disneyland. Level Two: Statue of Liberty. Level Three: Mount Rushmore. Level Four: Bok Tower Gardens. Level Five: Garden of Eden. Much of this book is written for people who want to know what happens beyond level five.)

The Bible speaks of a garden before it speaks of houses, so it seems reasonable to begin in the beginning with the Garden of Eden. This is not the one that was to be found between the Tigris and the Euphrates, but the one in Lawrence, Kansas, and it was inhabited not by Adam and Eve, but by a Samuel P. Dinsmoor. Dinsmoor's Garden of Eden was constructed largely of concrete poured between 1907 and 1929. He started his work at the age of sixty-four and continued through until five years before his death at eighty-nine. In 1927 he wrote a history of his "Cabin Home in the Garden of Eden," in which he described the place modestly enough as "the most unique home, for living or dead, on earth. Call and see it." In 1912 the arrival of Arizona and New Mexico into the Union drove him to erect a concrete Stars and Stripes, and he argued for its federal adoption—"It would stand out in all kinds of weather"— although later he was disillusioned by the government represented by Old Glory. "That flag protects capital today better than it does humanity. It drafted the boys but asked the money to volunteer. See the difference?"

But what about level-one attractions like Disneyland? How did they come about? Disneyland has inspired theme parks all over the world, but what inspired Disneyland? The answer may lie buried in a Florida backwood in Volusia County, not fifty miles from Orlando, where James N. Gamble, of Proctor and Gamble, built himself a "cracker" house in 1907. The house was more of a base for sporting recreation than for living in. Day visitors included President Taft, John D. Rockefeller, and H. J. Heinz. Gamble's adopted daughter, Maud, married a Cincinnati judge, Alfred Nippert, and they too loved the remote little house on Spruce Creek. When Maud died in 1937 Nippert needed something to concentrate on to excise his grief. In December he saw the movie sensation of the year, *Snow White and the Seven Dwarfs*, the first full-length feature cartoon. Nippert fell in love—not with Snow White, but with the seven dwarfs' house. Entranced, he sent his carpenter, Ernie Whidmeir, to sit through umpteen showings at the Daytona Beach Theater to get the architectural specifications. Day after day the carpenter sat in the darkened theater, surrounded by awestruck chidren. Whether the movie was too moving for him we'll never know, but the exercise failed and instead Nippert somehow managed to obtain some of the the original cels from the film. Working from the cels Whidmeir

Alfred Nippert's
replica of
Disney's seven
dwarfs' house is
a real-life sound
stage for a
cartoon.

produced a full-size replica of the seven dwarfs' house in under
three months, set in the woods of the Gamble House along Spruce
Creek. The film premiered on December 21, 1937, and Nippert's
seven dwarfs' house was completed on March 16, 1938. It was not
just thrown together; it was superbly built, right down to sash windows that drop into the walls, still working perfectly today. Some
changes had to be made—a thatched roof and earthen walls in
Florida would become a haven for bugs in a few hours, so the house
has a cedar shingle roof and log cabin sides, but the interior is as
close as you can get. This raises a philosophical point: which is the
real seven dwarfs' house? One is tangible, it exists in time and space,
but the original exists only on film. It never was. The house at
Spruce Creek is interactive. You can walk into it, and at the top of
the split log stairs are the headboards of each of the seven dwarfs'
beds, the fireplace is just as exaggeratedly massive as in the film, the
locks and door handles are beautifully made from the ubiquitous
Florida cypress knees. The ensemble is an uncannily accurate repre-
sentation of a fantasy, a real-life sound stage for a cartoon. Enthused
by success, Nippert went on to build a witch's hut from the hollow
trunk of a dead cypress, with a cutout of the wicked witch inside,
and a little way to the east a two-story rustic tower over the dwarfs'

diamond mine. There is no shaft—that would be stretching fantasy a little too far—and with true American practicality the ground floor of the tower concealed a cistern, but the upper floor was designed as a playhouse for Nippert's nieces and nephews. The seven dwarfs' house was a playhouse for the judge, not for children.

When this private, miniature theme garden was all complete Judge Nippert invited Walt Disney himself to visit. Disney came, saw, and went away impressed. He sent Nippert life-size models of Snow White and the seven dwarfs to enhance the house, and he must have started to think . . . Could it be that this little, half-forgotten folly buried deep in the backwoods was the inspiration behind Orlando's tourist millions?

There's no shaft underneath, but this rustic tower matches the one above the dwarfs' diamond mine in the Disney film.

The men who planned and built Holy Land USA as a theme park on the top of Pine Hill in Waterbury, Connecticut, insisted that they wished to remain anonymous. They pledged to maintain the services and utilities at the "village" at their own cost, but they did not have the money and power of a Gamble or a Disney. Despite the anonymity, it is readily apparent from the style, layout, and feel that this was the work of one man, and so it proves. John B. Greco, a Waterbury attorney, was the driving force and inspiration behind the park. Holy Land USA consists of scattered collections of small, crude model houses of a faintly Middle Eastern appearance, representing Jerusalem, Bethlehem, Nazareth, and other towns and villages from biblical Israel, interspersed with roughly made texts, largely exhortative, from the Bible. It is earnest, honest, passionate work, where the importance of the message far outstrips the competence of the craftsmanship. The result is a touching, affecting, naive innocence; awful and pathetic in the original true senses of those words. The whole place is so badly done, yet so genuine in its emotion, that it is very hard not to be moved by it. Its current state of dereliction only adds to the pathos.

The reinforced concrete statues in Antone Merton's religious park hardly inspire reverence.

ARCHITECTURAL FOLLIES IN AMERICA

There is a proper time to visit and appreciate all of these parks and gardens. Antone Merton's religious park 3,000 feet up in the desert at Yucca Valley, California, looks flat, odd, and lifeless, as if Magritte had caught religion and whitewashed his dreams. The park consists of larger-than-life reinforced concrete statues, painted in glittering gloss white, depicting scenes in the life of Jesus. But in harsh daylight the sense of wonder that the park is intended to instill is missing, and instead the groupings look childish and damaged, routinely standing among the yuccas, motionless and emotionless. The same park, seen in the black of night in a heavy thunderstorm, occasionally letting a flash of lightning illuminate the figures—now there would be an impressive and reverential sight.

The Reverend Howard Finster built his Paradise Garden, or Plant Farm Museum, in Summerville, Georgia, in 1905. One wonders how such passionate self-expression could possibly have been conveyed before the rediscovery of concrete, which Finster used in great flowing sweeps, embedding tiles and glass and junk and the Gospel and *objets trouvé* in it, and topping it off with turrets and pinnacles, a hymn evocatively frozen in gravel.

HISTORY OF PLANT FARM MUSEUM—IT TOOK ME ABOUT SEVEN YEARS TO CLEAR OUT THIS JUNGLE KILLING OVER ONE HUNDRED snakes and cutting thousands of trees, bushes, vines and thorns. Filling ditches. Leveling, cleaning out garbage throughout. Labor all by hand tools. Standing on mud palets raking out water ways for three spring branches. It was said by Mrs. C. L. Lowery that this place once was a lake where men hunted ducks from small rowe boats. Mr. C. L. Lowery former owner of this land dug into a clay pot of Indian arrow heads. If he found other things, its unknown. Since that time I found one small piece of yellow gold shining from the mud where I was digging, not too far from the claypot. Mr. Lowery was a music teacher wrote the words to the song Lifes Evening Sun. Allso studied and worked on prepitual machine 40 years, I now have remains of this machine. Many years ago I know God spoke to my soul that there was something for me in Pennville after 40 years preaching the gospel with out charge, I then felt led to build a paradise garden in which I will open print the holy Bible verse by verse, throughout, please respect for Christ sake.
—W. H. F.

Watching the progression of a folly garden is not dissimilar to watching "Old Faithful" erupt. The drive to convey a message bubbles and steams and belches along until inarticulacy explodes into architecture. The artists often start by expressing themselves in words, Biblical quotations, homilies, or proverbs, daubed in haste on any available surface: scrap metal, wood, doors, hoardings, anything that provides an accessible surface. Almost invariably the constraints of language finally prove too stifling to convey the required message and the silence of architecture becomes the medium of expression. It was ever thus; the decipherment of Linear-B allowed us to read Minoan inventories and shopping lists, but it was their architecture that spoke volumes.

Charley Kasling had a message to convey, and he chose statuary for his medium. He retired from the Navy in 1947 and went to the California desert for his health. There he made himself a garden and peopled it with ancient gods, characters from the Bible, famed prospectors, warriors, and historical tableaux, made from concrete or carved from sandstone and driftwood. He built long, elegant drystone walls, altars, plinths, at least one pyramid, and everywhere there were statues including (not unreasonably) one of himself. He cultivated yuccas, aloes, and saguaros, and tended his little corner of the desert with care and devotion. Charley died in Tucson in 1984, as old as the century, and now his garden has almost all disappeared, all but the impressive drystone walls and the desert plants left still standing in silent testimony to Driftwood Charley's lost garden. Fragments remain buried in the desert brush in back of the Sleepy Hollow RV Park on the Fort Yuma Indian Reservation at Andrade, on the Mexican border. The Quechan Indians own the territory, which is populated by quails and snowbirds. The tiny border road is choked with RVs lining up to cross into Los Algodones for cheap teeth and eyeglasses. Hidden from the road and far from the thoughts of the snowbirds lie these pathetic scraps of passion and patriotism. "God Bless America" reads Driftwood Charley's sole surviving inscription.

With equal fervor Romano Gabriel set about ornamenting his yard in Eureka to make the finest flower garden in northern California. The trouble was that, "Eureka bad place for flowers," as Gabriel succinctly put it. This was not strictly fair, as Eureka has a mild if rainy climate with no more than a ten-degree temperature variation throughout the year, from cool to very cool. Nevertheless this would not do for the Italian immigrant, doubtless accustomed

The saguaros stand in silent testimony to Driftwood Charley's lost garden.

to sunnier climes. He fabricated his flowers out of wooden crates and packing boxes, which he then painted in rich, patriotic American red, white, and blue and patriotic Italian red, white, and green. Some of his wilder flowers reached heights of twenty feet. When Gabriel died in 1977 his garden was declared a state landmark. This caused a problem in that nobody wanted to buy a house that was totally obscured by wooden flowers, so a solution had to be found. The garden was uprooted and transferred in its entirety to a downtown location on Second Street, where it is viewable all year round,

Architectural Follies in America

set in a purpose-built room with a glass wall fronting the street. Its preservation is admirable, and this is a solution of a sort, but by compressing the garden so it all fits within the available window space removes the magic and mystery of the actual garden and lends it the air of a fashionably naive window display in some tony Rodeo Drive boutique. No, I haven't any suggestions as to what else could have been done. Should you decide to visit the replica bottle house in Calico, California, you will pass Possom Trot in Yermo, a garden filled with wooden dolls of every size including "Often Seen Jim and his Limb." Worth a detour just for the name.

The classic garden building has little of the folly about it. Although it is a building for pleasure before purpose, which generally serves as a reasonable guide as to what is and is not a folly, there is nothing of the air of eccentricity that singles out the true folly. A summerhouse or gazebo is a practical if luxurious addition to a private garden; they are not usually follies. Thus it is interesting to find a few eccentric examples, some dating to the early years of the nation.

Life in seventeenth- and eighteenth-century America was rather more arduous than in the Old World. There was little time to indulge in frivolities in the garden, few leisurely afternoons to be spent sipping tea and watching the hunt from comfortable towers. In 1794 the United States of America was still a gawky adolescent, nervous at the prospect of a looming war with Britain. But in Salem, Massachusetts, the fortunes of Elias Harket Derby had scarcely suffered in the turbulent times. Whether in emulation of the English country estates, or to disprove rumors of his financial precariousness, or simply out of a sense of fun, Derby decided to build himself a teahouse on his estate. And what a teahouse! As his architect he employed Samuel McIntire, who had recently just missed out on the commission for the Capitol. McIntire knew the rules, but he played with them rather than by them. He produced a hidden masterpiece, a tiny two-story teahouse with all the classical conventions correctly copied but rearranged with a truly American disregard for convention. The life-size wooden statues of the milkmaid and farmboy,

The Derby-McIntire teahouse, a milkmaid perched on its pediment, wears its venerable age with grace and ease.

perched on each pediment, were carved by John and Simeon Silkin of Boston. The result is a really beautiful building that deserves to be famous. It graced the Derby estate for 107 years until it was purchased by Mrs. William Crowninshield Endicott, Sr., and reerected at The Farm in Danvers, ten miles away. The Farm is now called Glen Magna, and the old Derby-McIntire teahouse, set square like a little Ionic temple on a plinth, pristine and glittering white and looking nearer two than two-hundred years old, is the pride and joy of the Danvers Historical Society. It is an astonishing survival, almost as old as the country, and its survival should be taken as a symbol of America's recognition of the importance of architectural heritage. It wears its venerable age with grace and ease. There is no garden building of equal importance in America.

There was an older garden building, however, built in Annapolis, Maryland, and it can still be seen. The Paca Pavilion was built in the garden of 186 Prince George Street in 1763 by William Paca, a signatory of the Declaration of Independence and one-time governor of Maryland. Time and development are equally debilitating, and by 1965 the once-fine formal Paca gardens were buried under a parking lot, a bus station, and a hotel. Historic Annapolis, an action group under the leadership of Saint Clair Wright, campaigned for the state to buy the property and set about restoring—some would say over-restoring—the garden. It is now a perfect 1969 interpretation of a grand eighteenth-century garden and, as such, attracts its critics, who forget that without the impetus provided by Ms. Wright and her colleagues, there would now be a high-rise on the site. The little white pavilion is two storied, a domed hexagon on a square base, and all that remained in the 1960s were the traces of the foundations. The building we see today is the creation of landscape architect Laurance Brigham, and is modeled on similar-sized European garden pavilions of the time.

Gazebos and summerhouses were always popular in the settled Old World; the driving, impatient settlers of the New World were not so predisposed to contemplation and serenity. Nineteenth-century Pennsylvania, however, was about as settled and civilized as one could get in the New World around that time, and it is there that we find what is visually the nearest thing in America to a genuine European garden folly. Just north of Philadelphia on the grounds of the estate called Andalusia, on the banks of the Delaware River, stands a curious little Gothic building, like a sham ruined church. It is called the Grotto, and it was built between 1834 and 1836 for Nicholas

Biddle by Thomas U. Walter, as "a retiring room for the ladies." Biddle, who was president of the Second Bank of the United States (on the construction of which Walter had worked as an apprentice bricklayer), had employed Walter to add a great hexastyle Doric portico to Andalusia. The plans for the Grotto still exist, showing the tower that was never built. Walter and Biddle obviously had great fun creating this building as light relief from the authoritative Greek Revival style at which Walter excelled.

A particularly rare and fine hexagonal example of a garden building as a *garçonnière* can be found at the Burnside House in Houma, Louisiana. The garçonnières of nineteenth-century Louisiana were retiring rooms—although usually cocklofts above the main house—that were specifically set aside for maturing boys, away from the curious eyes of their younger siblings or the horrified glances of maiden aunts. Pubescent boys were translated from the family environment and left to erupt through adolescence in solitude. This is a custom well worth reviving.

Professional gazebo status can really only be awarded to buildings with more than four sides, although there is a pair of very early four-gabled Gothic exceptions to be found at Temelec in Sonoma,

California. Temelec is now an adult community, where only people over fifty-five years old are allowed to buy. Hidden among the repetitive crescents of similar houses is Temelec Hall, built in 1858 by Granville P. Swift, a member of the Bear Flag Party. It is a refined, colonnaded two-story mansion, used as the country club for the development, and just down from the house are these elegant little summerhouses, built of dressed black stone with white quoins, overlooking the remains of a small formal garden now invaded by a swimming pool. One house is now used as a little workshop, the other shelters lawn mowers from the torrential rain. Octagonal gazebos are too numerous to list so one will stand for all, hard by the road on the eastern outskirts of Charleston, West Virginia, just curious enough to snap the head round while passing. No peace, no solitude there; it had to predate the road.

This four-gabled Gothic gazebo at Temelec Hall is one of a pair.

As America flexed its financial muscles and money became no object in the late nineteenth century, the new millionaires turned to architecture to relieve the burden of wealth, as so many had done before them. The "cottages" in Newport, Rhode Island, palaces to we ordinary mortals, herd together along Bellevue Avenue against the common hordes as if aware that they, too, were as endangered as the bison. To European eyes the gardens in which these mansions are set seem pitifully small, all heart and no lungs. We arrived too early in the morning to be admitted to The Elms, so we followed the catering van in and drove around to the back, where we found two teahouses on the grounds, ornate little garden pavilions dimly glimpsed through the downpour as guards squished across the sodden lawn to tell us what we already knew. There is something about rain and gazebos that goes together well. Down the road, Marble House has a Chinese teahouse overlooking the sea. More interesting and much less known in the same state is a pavilion erected to the memory of a favorite cow at North Farm in Bristol, "America's Most Patriotic City" (the double lines in the middle of the road are painted red, white, and blue). Pleasant and unremarkable save for its raison d'etre, the Cow Pavilion now stands on the grounds of a condominium.

Did Columbus have a beard? This burning question was the cause of years of argument between the sculptor Ferdinand Miller and his client Henry Shaw. Shaw commissioned Miller to cast a bronze statue of the politically challenged explorer to enhance his Tower Grove Park, formerly a prairie on the edge of the village of Saint Louis, Missouri. Shaw had begun landscaping his park in 1868, by which time Saint Louis was something more than a village. Realizing that any decent park was much more than an assemblage of interesting plants and trees, he commissioned architects and sculptors to frame and decorate the park. His great achievement was to produce the first authentic sham ruin in America, a country crying out for decent ruins. In 1867 Saint Louis had for four years been the proud possessor of the country's largest hotel, the Lindell on sixth and Washington streets. Designed by Thomas Walsh, it had taken seven years to build; that year it burned down. Shaw acquired blocks of the elaborately carved, smoke-blackened, water-hosed limestone, and with the help of his gardener, James Gurney, assembled two ruins in the best English landscape garden tradition. They are not, sadly, great

works of art—a century earlier an architectural critic had com-
mented that building a ruin was not as easy as it looked:

> There is great art, and difficulty also in creating a building
> of this kind. It is not every man, who can build a house,
> that can execute a ruin. To give the stone it's mouldering
> appearance—to make the widening chink run naturally
> through all the joints—to mutilate the ornaments—to
> peel the facing from the internal structure—to shew how
> correspondent parts have once united; tho now the chasm
> runs wide between them—and to scatter heaps of ruin
> around with negligence and ease; are great efforts of art;
> much too delicate for the hand of a common workman;
> and what we very rarely see performed.
>
> Besides, after all that art can bestow, you must put
> your ruin at last into the hands of nature to adorn, and

America cries out
for decent ruins,
and Henry Shaw
did the country a
favor by
commissioning its
first authentic
fake.

perfect it. If the mosses, and lychens grow unkindly on your walls—if the streaming weather-stains have produced no variety of tints—if the ivy refuses to mantle over your buttress; or to creep among the ornaments of your Gothic window—if the ash, cannot be bought to hang from the cleft; or long, spiry grass to wave over the shattered battlement—your ruin will be still incomplete—you may as well write over the gate, Built in the year 1772. Deception there can be none.

—William Gilpin,
Observations Relative Chiefly to Picturesque Beauty, 1772

Shaw's ruin is much too neat and ordered; there is no mystery or imagination about it. But facing it in the Sailboat Pond is a stroke of genius: a three-tiered fountain painted a particularly repellent pale turquoise is perched on a false island made out of all the really interesting carved scraps of capitals, cartouches, entablatures, and other architectural detritus taken from the ruined hotel. This architectural island is unique in the country and, as far as I know, in the world. It is rather prettily floodlit at night, lessening the impact of the color scheme.

But I digress. What about Columbus's beard? The statue of Columbus in front of the Coit Tower in San Francisco is clean-shaven. Shaw, a clean-shaven man, was adamant that he was bearded; Miller was equally convinced of the opposite. You will have already realized that the wishes of the client always take precedence over those of the artist: the Columbus statue in Tower Grove Park has a full Old Testament beard. Miller still felt strongly about the matter. Hidden under Christopher's cloak is a disclaimer signed by the artist, refusing all responsibility for the offending whiskers.

At the Boothe Memorial Park in Stratford, Connecticut, the eccentricity comes not just from the individual buildings but from their juxtaposition. Two brothers, David and Stephen Boothe, built a summer cottage in their backyard. Summer cottages are usually located hundreds of miles away from the year-round home, not a hundred yards away on the same property, but nothing the Boothes did was conventional. They began their park in 1913. The Clock Tower Museum is the most eccentric building of the lot; the Technocratic Cathedral is soberly described in the National Register inventory as "very idiosyncratic in design." David Boothe, on hearing that Henry Ford had only built a humdrum four-sided, four-cornered blacksmith's shop, bragged that his blacksmith's shop had a much more interesting total of forty-four sides, which it does by means of a convoluted array of false buttresses disguising a humdrum four-sided blacksmith's shop. The brothers built a leaning tower, "neither round, nor square, nor plumb," (it was actually octagonal) that took to its role with too much enthusiasm and is consequently no longer with us. The top of Stratford lighthouse replaced the leaning tower, a suitably Boothelike addition. "Fancy architects have come to gawk, and we never went to architecture school," boasted the Boothes.

Along the Connecticut coast in Greenwich two outbuildings dating from the 1920s and 1930s on the John D. Chapman estate on Round Island exhibited whimsy almost worthy of the Boothes. The Lodge was a five-car garage stone built with the upper story timber framed and filled with wattle and daub. This really was harking back to the Old World, and the addition of a staircase tower in the shape of a Kentish oast completes the regression. It is now a separate house. A beach pavilion on the shore is disguised as a sham ruined monastery, with heavy buttresses, an uneven roof line, and arched walls. Used brick and imported stone were employed by architect Spencer Guidal to create the effect.

Many of the folly sites found in America come with gardens of equal perplexity and merit, sometimes bundled with their more famous partners, sometimes waiting quietly in the wings for recognition. Tom Kelly's bottle house in Rhyolite, Nevada, has a strange little garden built by Kelly's successor "Tommy" Thompson. It is a crude model in cement and glass of the houses in the ghost town, protected by a fence made from broken bottle necks strung along a wire, glinting and turning in the sunshine. There is a rock garden behind the Desert Watch Tower at Jacumba Hot Springs, California, but it is unlike any rock garden you might expect. An engineer by the name of W. T. Ratcliffe arrived in the area in the early 1930s and took a liking to the large boulders tumbled around the tower. He discovered that they lent themselves well to carving and, inspired by their prehistoric waterworn shapes, he proceeded to adapt them here and there to create a petrified menagerie. Over a period of three years he carved a turtle, a Gila monster, a fish, a coiled rattlesnake, a buffalo, a crested lizard, a dinosaur, a huge skull with grinning white teeth—a monster from *Sesame Street* forty years before its time, an alligator facing off a lizard, the head of an Indian, and more. At first

Petrified menagerie: Above and below, W. T. Ratcliffe adapted desert boulders' natural contours to create bizarre animals and a huge, grinning skull.

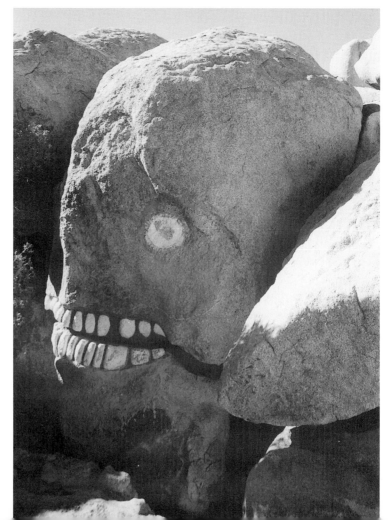

they are difficult to make out in the blinding white desert light, then suddenly they leap into three dimensions. In some cases mouths and eyes are daubed with red and white paint for emphasis. The alligator is only completed on one side; perhaps Ratcliffe died or he simply lost interest and wandered on. It is a bizarre assembly. A few miles southwest of Redmond, Oregon, is another strange rock garden, this one created by a Danish immigrant to America in 1906. Rasmas Petersen spent seventeen years building bridges, castles, terraces, towers, ponds, and mansions out of exotic sounding rocks and stones like obsidian and agate.

The area around Grant's Tomb at the end of 122nd Street in Manhattan is covered with a fanfare of colored tiles and mosaics, applied not just to the benches but also to the weird, twisted, convoluted pillars of concrete that entwine the benches and the formal area surrounding the gigantic mausoleum. The colorful but anachronistic project was started by a Chilean artist, Pedro Silva, who had been inspired by Anton Gaudí's Benches of Barcelona. It became a public arts scheme, and was designed and carried out by local people, from children to senior citizens. Against the solemn grandeur of architect John Duncan's reinterpretation of the Tomb of

Pedro Silva's mosaic fanfare provides a jarring counterpoint to the staid grandeur of Grant's Tomb.

King Mausolus at Halicarnassus, the festive benches provide a pleasantly jarring counterpoint. A survey carried out by the park rangers who work at the tomb showed that 50 percent of visitors liked the benches, 30 percent disliked them, and 20 percent thought them "inappropriate to surround a national monument of such stature as Grant's Tomb."

A sizeable garden unrelieved by architecture will be poorly planned; all ordered landscapes benefit from buildings. Throughout America, all the great gardens will have structures where one can rest and appreciate the surroundings, from the studied informality of a rustic, thatched summerhouse built by Theodore Wirth in 1903 in the rose garden of Elizabeth Park in West Hartford, Connecticut, to the faux-Tudor half-timbering of Edsel Ford's children's playhouse at Grosse Pointe, Michigan, or the austere formality of Alfred Victor du Pont and Gabriel Massena's gloriette and tower at Nemours, Delaware, constructed in the 1930s.

One might think that the days of sustained garden architecture were passing, if not already over, so it is startling and exciting to discover in Ohio a substantial collection of recent garden buildings, including giocchi d'acqua, a nymphaeum, guest room, grotto, sham ruin, bridge, and torrent. The follies have been created over a period of twenty years in a secluded garden outside Cincinnati by Theodore Gantz for his patron. At the head of a small lake a pavilion flanks a stream, on the other side of which a ruined wall closes the view. Scraps of half-remembered building jut out of the crumbled masonry, years of building upon building stretching back over the centuries—one-fifth of a century in this case. A delightful septagonal room lit from above has the skull of a unicorn to detain the visitor momentarily before crossing a tiny covered bridge to a guest bedroom. This is where the fun begins—outside, the courtyard is paved with tiny pebbles, a mosaic of red, white, and gray, fronting a nymphaeum from which water flows. Linger too long, however, and your host will be tempted to pull a hidden lever. The paved courtyard explodes into a dozen fountains, drenching the hapless visitor. This is a very old joke, popular in sixteenth-century Italy, and still not remotely amusing. With dampened enthusiasm we descend a couple of steps into a grotto cavern. To the left and right are thunder rooms, tiny circular chambers in which the waters from the dammed-up stream beyond drop a mere eight feet or so—but the volume as they fall is deafening, cleverly amplified by the acoustic shape of the little recesses. The earth seems to shift under the force of the torrent; minutes ago and yards away you were dry, warm, and comfortable. Niches at the side of the facing wall let in to a lenticular room with a large fountain in front. Pressed wetly against the back wall you are by now soaked and ready for just about anything, except for the size of the spider crouching just above your head, with a good six-foot leg span. Chuckling malevolently, your host reaches up and yanks a leg. Slowly, the great clamshell in front of you opens and Venus emerges, flanked by dolphins guardant. Transfixed, you await the inevitable, and inexorably it comes. Jets of water shoot out from every imaginable orifice and souse your feet. Very funny.

Chapter 7

SOLEMN
TEMPLES

The rotunda in Mount Storm Park, Cincinnati, is, properly speaking, a monopteros.

Nothing caught the imagination of American architects like the Greek Revival. The tetrastyle portico is such a popular motif that it could be taken as native to the United States. Its simple, classic elegance, its adaptability, its suitability for a climate similar to Greece in many parts, its authority—all these factors point to its success. There is now more Grecian architecture in America than there is in Greece.

The circular temple with six, eight, or ten columns supporting a dome can be found everywhere. Properly called a monopteros, there are examples in every state: the bandstand temple on the Common in Boston; the Love Temple in the beautiful Longwood Gardens in Kennet Square, Pennsylvania; the Doric-domed rotunda in George Rogers Clark National Historic Park in Vincennes, Indiana; the thin, pale example allegedly made from tin in Mount Storm Park overlooking Cincinnati—there are too many to count. Someone, someday, will make a register of them.

The Parthenon, that symbol of Athens, is not the magnificent temple it once was. It has never really recovered from being blown up in the seventeenth century when the Turks were using it as an arsenal. All the color and painting has disappeared, as has the roof and most of the interior, Athenians have used it as a convenient quarry—it's in a sorry state. If you want to see it in its true glory, however, there is no need to make that tedious transatlantic journey: a much brighter, newer, and perhaps slightly bigger version can be found in Nashville, Tennessee. The Museum of Art in Philadelphia, Pennsylvania, is on a similar scale, built in 1928 above the Schuylkill River with pavilions below echoing the Greek theme, but added by the Fairmount Water Works.

SOLEMN TEMPLES

149

What the Greeks gave the world were themes. The Temple of the Winds in Athens was not a temple but a water clock, and its satisfying octagon shape with two porticos has been copied and echoed around the western world. Richard Franklin Sammons, a young New York architect, borrowed the theme for a gardener's house he designed for an estate in Virginia in 1993, while Jones and Herrin, a practice in Huntsville, Alabama, produced a classic copy of the severe little Temple of Ceres for a client in northern Florida who wanted something, but wasn't quite sure what. Now that it has been built, the owner thinks he may sit in it and read. Decisions, decisions. The same practice added a Roman façade to the side of a garage in their hometown, providing a stage-set sham temple to screen the view of the garage from the main 1854 house. There is even a Temple of Convenience: behind a house in Georgetown, Colorado, is an authentic Greek Revival temple as a privy, a six-holer no less, with cupola, cornice, and porch, designed by W. A. Hammill in the 1880s. Brendan Gill, that mainstay of the *New Yorker*, listed the "pillared Palladian folly on West 57th Street leading into the Parker-Meridien Hotel" as one of his twenty-four Bests of New York.

Daniel Burnham's precept to "make no little plans" has been followed avidly throughout America. In 1922 the city fathers of Lakeland in Florida wanted something to distinguish their town, and they found it in state legislator Thomas W. Bryant. When Henry Plant's new railroad steamed through Polk County in 1884, the sleepy farming community of Lakeland suddenly had the opportunity to reach export markets. The little settlement prospered and became a small town. The small town boomed, and became a city. Funds were raised to finance urban development, for roads, utilities, and the purchase of Lake Mirror in the center of the city. In 1926 Bryant wrested approval for the construction of a colonnaded promenade around Lake Mirror from a reluctant chamber of commerce, who already saw the end of the boom in sight. Work started, to the designs of Charles W. Leavitt, in 1927. The stock market crash was looming, but building was completed by April 1928. Lakeland then had the magnificent Lake Mirror Promenade and a massive debt. There is a mighty loggia at the head of the lake, and a colonnaded walkway encircling it; the effect is Pompeiian on a grand scale. It is startling to come across this jewel in what would otherwise be the fading decay of a typical American downtown, and its existence and recent renovation has stimulated the city to a general restoration and rejuvenation.

Debts are paid, amortised, defaulted upon, lost, settled, and forgotten about, but a sweeping architectural statement like the columns at Lakeland will speak for the city long after the folly of its overstretched financial resources has been forgotten.

Southern Minnesota has a hideous temple monument to Hermann the German, built by Julius Berndt in 1897. This is not a Teutonic joke; there really was a Hermann the German and he was a big hero to the German-speaking settlers of New Ulm. The round temple, set on a high plinth, is irredeemably ugly, with an iron staircase wandering about uncertainly before it finally realizes it has to reach the ceiling, on the dome of which stands a 32-foot statue of Hermann wielding a sword. Hermann was the leader of the Cherusci tribe who unified Germans in 9 A.D. and drove the Romans back across the Rhine. Nearly 2,000 years later a monument is erected half a world away.

The Greeks and the Romans never had a monopoly on temples, however. Their style may have been all pervasive, but the architecture of other creeds is equally majestic. I have yet to discover the stupendous stupas of Angkor Wat in America, but a charming little sandstone Hindu temple sits on the campus at Florida Southern College in Lakeland, the gift of Bishop Frederick Fisher. Fisher went as a missionary to India and managed to convert an entire village, including the Hindu priest. The bishop then climbed the village temple and placed a cross on top. He ordered a replica of the temple from Benares to commemorate this startling event, and had it shipped to Massachusetts. One month before he died in 1936, Fisher visited the Florida Southern campus and offered the temple to the college. The tiny 25-foot high temple, set in its own little garden at

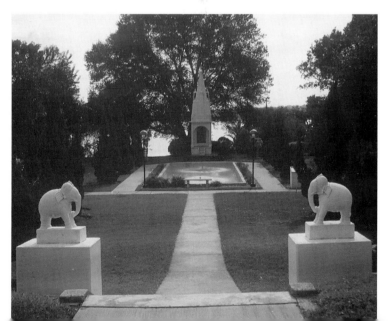

The little Hindu temple at Florida Southern College has room inside for one worshiper.

The domes on the Vedanta Center's roof architecturally acknowledge the world's major religions.

the head of a reflecting pool, has room for one Hindu worshiper or two or three friendly nonworshipers. It is rather overwhelmed by the half-dozen or so Frank Lloyd Wright buildings on campus, so someone decided to paint it white to make it more prominent.

Stupas are suggested by the multidomed, oxblood-colored roof of the Vedanta Center's Old Temple at Webster and Filbert Streets in San Francisco. Admired even by natives, it is a miniature Kremlin below Pacific Heights, designed by the leader of the sect Swami Trigunatitananda with the architect Joseph A. Leonard. It was built in 1905, surviving the 1906 earthquake, and the thinking behind its onion dome (orthodox Christianity), Moorish dome (Islam), and remarkable Jain-inspired cluster of spired domes (Hindu) is that Vedanta teachings acknowledge all the world's major religions. It now describes itself as spiritually affiliated with the Ramakrishna Order.

The World's Largest Jigsaw Puzzle can be found near Greynolds Park, north of Miami. The Church of Saint Bernard de Clairvaux is a chapel and cloister without a monastery. It was bought at a cost of half a million dollars from Segovia, Spain, in 1925 by William Randolph Hearst, and was intended to surround the Neptune swimming pool at his San Simeon home. Unfortunately the 11,000 numbered crates containing the cloisters were impounded in New York by the Department of Agriculture due to an outbreak of hoof-and-mouth disease in Segovia; the crates were broken open and the hay cushioning the stones was taken out and burned. The stones were then put back in the wrong crates. Hearst understandably lost interest. In 1952 the boxes were bought by two businessmen who intended the cloisters to be a tourist attraction. They shipped the crates to Miami and spent nineteen months and $1.5 million figuring out how to reassemble the stones. Eventually they sold the partially reconstructed cloisters (there are a whole bunch of stones at the back that don't seem to fit anywhere) to the Episcopalians who now use it as a conventional church. Surrounded and shaded by venerable banyan trees, it is a favorite spot for Cuban brides to be photographed in their wedding finery.

It took nineteen months and $1.5 million to put the Church of Saint Bernard of Clairvaux back together again—almost.

Chapter 8

THE GREAT GLOBE ITSELF

nglish is an extraordinary language. There are two words for practically everything. It's like playing an organ with two keyboards, one Latin and one Old English. So a grotto is a cave and a cave is a grotto, and over the years they have acquired shades of meaning that allow us to differentiate between two manifestations of the same thing. The Catholic Church sees a grotto as a quasi-religious shrine, whereas garden historians see it as a decorated cave. To the Catholic hierarchy, grottoes figure largely as a gentle form of self-expression by the people, a little leeway from a closely observed rite.

Napoleon Pelletier was born in Canada in 1857. He and a group of fellow Catholics would travel to Lake Wales in central Florida to escape the crisp and even Canadian winters, and they brought their deep faith with them. In 1921 they built a small white church five miles out of town, and Napoleon was driven to erect a great grotto apse, flanked by small arches, dedicated to Saint Anne. The reverent little community lasted until the outbreak of World War II, when Pelletier died. The tiny shrines, fountains, and altars gently decayed, until a suspiciously commercial revival in the 1950s again brought the site to the attention of the diocese. There was talk of miracle cures, and money changing hands, and 75,000 visitors in a year. It had to be stopped. The bishop of Florida ordered it to be closed; the church was torn down and the grotto cleared of its revered artifacts. Saint Anne Shrine is now a peaceful lakeside community, but at the foot of the lake remains a peculiar cone-shaped structure built of rubbly stone, and a rustic bridge, and deeper into the wood comes the shock of this towering grotto apse, lurking in

This peculiar structure is one of the few remains of the Saint Anne Shrine.

the undergrowth, still with pleas and prayers and offerings lying on its unofficial altar. There is also Pelletier's gravestone, but his body was removed long ago.

The most touching of all American grotto makers was James Hampton, an impoverished black man from Elloree, South Carolina. He worked as a short-order cook, got conscripted, was honorably discharged in 1945, and ended up in Washington, where he found work as a janitor. He rented a garage in the seedy neighborhood where he lived, and collected gold and silver foil. Nothing else was known about him; he had no friends to speak of. He spent all his spare time in his locked garage. Not until he died was his secret fully revealed. For fifteen years James Hampton had been building a throne for God in his garage, a glittering array of sedilia, lecterns, offertory tables, and pulpits, all girded with gold and silver foil, gleaming in the dull light. None of James's fellow humans had visited James in his garage, but God, Moses, Adam, and the Blessed Virgin Mary had been there.

Moving on to a more secular definition of the word, we encounter grottoes that incorporate a world of sea shells and snails, of water and whimsy. The great lexicographer Samuel Johnson remarked that "a grotto is a very fine place—for a toad," and it is certainly true that the best grottoes are cold, dank, damp places, or cool, fertile, watery havens, depending on your point of view. There has recently been an upswing of interest in decorative grottoes. As the heritage and conservation movement gains momentum in America, people with the specialist knowledge and skills needed to restore grottoes have found their services in demand not only for the renovation of public works but also for creating entirely new private grottoes. Two of the new grotto builders are Theodore Gantz from Cincinnati and Belinda Eade from London. Eade, in collaboration with the British sculptor Simon Verity, recently completed a substantial grotto in six months, working in a private garden designed by Bostonian Keith Leblanc in Fort Worth, Texas. Gantz has spent twenty years on a major project for a client in Ohio: a group of structures at the end of a large lake that incorporate a figure of Neptune with a trident, gravel and pebble gardens, a Tuscan farmhouse, *giocchi d'acqua* (water tricks that drench unwary visitors), and a shell grotto. A fuller description of this remarkable work can be found in the chapter on parks and gardens. Aurora, Indiana, has that rarest of garden delights, a prospect grotto. Just to the side of Hill Forest, a glorious Steamboat Gothic beauty built by Thomas Gaff in 1851, is a tiny grotto set in the steep hillside overlooking the Ohio River. On top are the remains of four little seats for drinking in the view, which now features an active petrochemical works belching out yellow smoke.

The Venetian Pool in Coral Gables, Florida, was originally a quarry from which limestone was hewn for house building. This left a great unsightly hole in the middle of an upmarket Miami suburb, so it was decided to fill it with water to make a vast swimming pool. Then, in 1924, Denman Fink had the idea of carving grottoes out of the coral rock, adding bridges, towers, and striped poles and creating an idealized Venetian lagoon, presumably without all the dead cats, stench, and streetwalkers of the original. This was used to pro-

mote the residential development, as it looked undeniably exotic, but people had to be paid to splash around in it: "I've never known water as cold, either as a child or an adult," said a local motel manager, "and I lived in Wisconsin for thirty years before coming back to Coral Gables." Seen on a muggy December morning, with tendrils of fog curling round the piscina poles, the huge, empty pool has an other-worldly look, deserted, mysterious, and magical.

By most accounts the first humans appeared to be cave dwellers, and some of us can't quite shake the habit. South of Moab, Utah, is the Home 'n' the Rock, a house carved into a large rock. This was surely not done to get away from it all, as it is alleged that the sign advertising the place can be seen from orbiting spacecraft. The inhabitants of Cave City, near the Mammoth Cave National Park in Kentucky, have exploited the natural local rock's propensity to form interesting holes by attracting tourists from all over to see if they really do lead a troglodytic existence. (They don't.)

Our ancestors may well have been cave dwellers, but they were just as likely to have been tree dwellers. The thought of an arboreal existence has a certain seductive charm. I have yet to see a tree house in America although I have heard of several—Max Schroff's tree

Denman Fink transformed an unsightly quarry hole into the mysterious and magical Venetian Pool.

The Stump House, in Eureka, has been selling souvenirs since 1902.

house dating from the 1880s in Rock River, Wisconsin; a tree house built by Morton B. Ewing forty feet up in a buttonwood tree in Hellam, Pennsylvania; and the John Frémont Redwood Tree House in Santa Cruz, California. In Hellam I was sidetracked by a house in the shape of a shoe and Ewing's tree house, if it still exists, remains to be discovered. There is a pleasant story about a guy in Athens, Georgia, who was particularly fond of one tree on his property. He made a will in favor of the tree, so now it is known as the Tree That Owns Itself. We usually expect tree houses to be perched among branches, but the California redwoods are so huge that it is theoretically possible to live inside one. In Eureka a deliberately different "house" was hollowed out of the stump of a giant redwood tree, lying on its side, along Highway 101. Known as Stump House, it has been a souvenir shop since 1902. The World Famous Tree House is five miles south of Piercy on the same road. Inside the living tree a space has been hollowed out to make a room 20 feet by 27 feet, and 50 feet high. The tree itself is 250 feet tall. The inside space has served as a barn, a blacksmith's shop, and sleeping quarters for thirty-two convicts. It used to be called the Fraternal Monarch, then the Quadruped Tree, but it has always been a tourist attraction.

ARCHITECTURAL FOLLIES IN AMERICA

The World Famous Tree House, near Piercy, California, has one very large room inside.

Arriving in Leggett to see the One Log House, another "house" hacked out of a redwood trunk, we discovered that, after a promotional tour around the country for the California Redwood Organization, it had been parked up in Phillipsville, forty miles north and through which we'd just come. So we comforted ourselves by seeing if a Lincoln Town Car could squeeze through the Chandelier Tree, on the theory that if you can get through a gap in a tree at six miles an hour, you can get through it at sixty. It could.

Baldasare Forestiere dug a tunnel 800 feet long that was wide enough for any Lincoln. He was an Italian immigrant from Messina, and he was America's greatest cave dweller. Forestiere, a small, spare, handsome man, came to the United States in 1901 at the age of twenty-two, and found work digging the subway in Boston or New York; accounts differ. In 1908 he arrived in Fresno, California, and purchased seventy acres of land at a very advantageous price, apparently without seeing it first, because when he came to take possession he discovered that an inch or two under the topsoil was nothing but hardpan, virtually solid chunks of rocklike soil, useless for growing things. He had been ripped off. There was too much Italian pride to admit to having made a mistake, so he thought for a while and then started to hack through the hardpan. Underneath he found good fertile soil. His solution was pure genius. He set to work digging out his house and garden completely underground, using the hardpan as a roof and cutting circular holes in it to allow for light, ventilation, and rain. By the time he died in 1946 he had constructed more than ninety underground rooms at 5021 West Shaw Avenue, using only his pick, shovel, and wheelbarrow. Ten

Baldasare Forestiere forsook a career in subway tunnels and dug himself a ninety-room underground house.

ARCHITECTURAL FOLLIES IN AMERICA

acres of patios, courts, archways, and grottoes are all linked by paths meandering through sunken gardens ten to twenty-five feet below ground. Citrus trees, some grafted to grow up to seven varieties of fruit from one stock, grow from pots carved in the underground chambers through holes in the hardpan roof artfully placed to catch the most beneficial sunlight and rainwater. Above ground you can pick oranges from the tops of trees. He had no explanation for his subterranean behavior, other than that Fresno got a little hot in the summer.

In Forestiere's sunken gardens, you can pick oranges from the tops of trees.

Forestiere worked at tremendous speed. As early as 1923 he had completed fifty rooms and his underground road for automobiles, which was 800 feet long. Plans were in place for a ballroom and an underground lake. He excavated all this. The ballroom, now floored with composite stone and covered by a large wooden roof, is vast. The lake is not; it is a circular room about ten feet in diameter with a hole in the roof to let in light and another hole about four feet wide in the middle of the floor. Below this is a small bell-shaped chamber with ledges on which you can sit. The idea was to cover the hole in the roof of the bell-shaped room with a sheet of glass, then fill the room above with water to make a shallow pond. You could then sit in the chamber below and watch the fish above, like an aquarium in the ceiling. Forestiere never completed his skylight aquarium, but it would not be expensive to finish it off. Unfortunately the owners, Baldasare's nephew Ricardo Forestiere and his wife Lorraine, simply haven't got the money. A lawsuit that has dragged on for eight years has kept these magical underground gardens permanently closed to visitors, depriving the Forestieres of their income. Such troubles are not unknown to these underground gardens. To keep up his work, Baldasare had to mortgage the property and in March, 1931, the mortgagees foreclosed. "I have been doing this for fun," he said at the time. "Money? What do I want with money? If I had $1 million I couldn't spend it. I am broke, but this cavern and all the work it represents is worth more than $1 million to me." He had to open the caves to visitors to raise funds. They have been opened and closed on and off ever since he started his work. At the time of writing they are closed for the foreseeable future; inquiries about their current status should be made to the Fresno Convention and Visitor's Bureau. One hopes that the city will recognize the treasure it has under its hardpan and spend the money necessary to preserve Forestiere's masterpiece. It is unique in California, unique in America, unique in the world.

Chapter 9

EYECATCHERS

Eyecatchers, buildings that served such a prominent role in the European landscape garden by focusing the attention and setting out the scene in the manner of a landscape painting, found little purchase in the American landscape—and reasonably enough, for the views available to the astonished eyes of the new Americans were quite grand enough to answer themselves. Indeed, almost every state can boast vistas of awesome grandeur. The appreciation of the sublime quality of a view is international. As a comfortable standard of living gradually replaced the bare struggle for survival, the wealthy tended to move out of the cities where they had made their money and settle in areas of scenic beauty. New Yorkers moved upstream and settled the banks of the Hudson, much as Londoners had with the Thames. But the Hudson is incomparably magnificent against London's dull but historic river. Frederick Church's house, Olana, is singled out here not because of its gorgeous polychromy or the fantasy eclecticism of its architecture, but because of its view, outstanding, breathtaking, all-

The fantasy eclecticism of Olana's architecture is outdone by the house's breathtaking view.

encompassing. What joy to rise in the morning and simply gaze on that majestic prospect. No need for artificial or architectural aids.

The purpose of an architectural eyecatcher is to enhance a view, to trick or surprise the viewer, to gild the lily. When that intention is there from the beginning it is hard to call it folly, but if it is inadvertent—the building imposing itself on our consciousness with a shock of misplaced recognition—there is a stronger case. Bridges, for example, are probably the most functional and utilitarian—and often the most beautiful—structures devised by man. Most animals make shelters, beavers even make dams, but only man builds bridges. And when a bridge fails to fulfill its function, when it becomes a mere architectural appendage, then its title as folly can scarcely be disputed.

Arizona has two folly bridges. North of Yuma, a town so warm that residents say, "If you're goin' to hell, be sure to take your blanket," the McPhaul Bridge, a fine suspension bridge, was built in 1929 at a cost

ARCHITECTURAL FOLLIES IN AMERICA

of $140,000 to cross the Gila River. But the river is seldom around nowadays and in any case the road has been diverted, so the bridge, an elegant prototype for the Golden Gate Bridge, flings the old State Road 95 impressively over 970 feet of near nothingness toward the temptingly named Chocolate Mountains. The desolate, abandoned bridge sings sadly to itself in the sunset. With traffic no longer crossing there is no variation of weight for the steel tensioning bars to take up; they expand in the heat of the sun and contract in the cool desert night, and as their day's work supporting the ghost of SR-95 comes to an end, they twang softly in the dusk like a forgotten guitar.

Carry on up the new Route 95 and you will be rewarded with a bridge that does cross water, although both the water and the bridge have been imported. The water comes from the reservoir created by the building of the Parker Dam. The bridge is London Bridge, at Lake Havasu City, Robert P. McCulloch's planned community. Together with his master planner, C. V. Wood Jr., who helped plan Disneyland, McCulloch decided to buy the old London Bridge in 1968 for nearly $2.5 million as a centerpiece for his community. The question has been asked time and time again—did they know what they were buying? The London Bridge of nursery rhyme and folklore has indeed fallen down several times over the centuries. The Romans were the first to bridge the Thames, 2,000 years ago, when the river was far wider than today. London Bridge was burned by a marauding Danish king in 980 A.D., destroyed again in 1090, burned down in 1135, condemned as unsafe in 1170, and eventually rebuilt in stone in 1176. This is the famous one, the one that lasted all the way to the nineteenth century, lined with dwellings and shops, like the Ponte Vecchio in Florence or the Rialto in Venice, but for nearly two centuries it has been a simple unadorned river crossing. The bridge that stands in splendor in the Arizona desert was built by John Rennie in 1831 and was replaced by an apology for a bridge that will not last 137 years, let alone 650. Never mind. In its new location, London Bridge originally crossed dry land, but McCulloch had a channel dug underneath it so it now traverses a shallow reach. It is not, as one might imagine, solely on display as the largest antique in the world, but is in everyday use as a four-lane road bridge, carrying McCulloch Boulevard over to Pittsburgh Point. Every Londoner is convinced that the "Yankees" (all Americans are Yanks to the Brits) thought they were buying Tower Bridge, the Victorian bascule marvel that has come to represent London in the way the Gateway Arch represents Saint Louis.

ARCHITECTURAL FOLLIES IN AMERICA

If pride is a motivation for builders, then how much stronger a motivation is civic or national pride? Can it be strong enough to build a stainless steel rainbow, higher than a fifty-story skyscraper? Yes. Eero Saarinen won the competition to design the Jefferson National Expansion Memorial in Saint Louis, Missouri, in 1948. The memorial, better known as the Gateway Arch, was completed in 1965, four years after Saarinen died, at a cost of $29 million; this in the city that built the Pruitt-Igoe development. The arch is 630 feet high and has an equal span, the tallest monument in the world; it is described as being "in the form of an inverted catenary curve," that is, if you take an utterly flexible rope and hang it from two points, this is the curve you will get—depending on the length of the rope and the distance between the points, of course. Outstanding for 1948; now every home computer can produce such curves ad infinitum.

"Make no little plans, for they have no magic to stir men's blood," wrote Daniel H. Burnham, Chicago's city planner after the Great Fire of 1872. It is a maxim that has served generations of Americans well. The Gateway Arch is the tallest monument in the world, but it is not the most massive. If you are going to build something to catch the eye, argued Boston sculptor Korczak Ziolkowski, you may as well make it grab the eye and shake it like a terrier. So, in 1947, he started to create the largest statue in the world. He took Thunderhead Mountain, in the Black Hills of South Dakota, and began blasting away anything that did not look like Crazy Horse on horseback. Ziolkowski died in 1982 but his work continues. One can now see most of Crazy Horse's head and part of his arm. This is going to make Mount Rushmore look like Toyland. The statue—the monolith—is 600 feet high. It would barely scrape under the Saint Louis Arch. Is it a folly? It will be if it's not completed, and that will be after our lifetimes.

Even if you are too young to remember "Kilroy Was Here" you would appreciate a series of bizarre works—not art, not architecture, but unusual enough to unnerve the unsuspecting driver—that crop up along the sides of U.S. Route 43 in Forkland, north of Demopolis, Alabama. Kilroy, a giant spider, a caterpillar, a dinosaur, a dragon, an octopus, a lady matador, a bull, Miss Piggy, an owl, a pussycat, and a locomotive, among other weird representations spring eerily up from the surrounding stubble, menacing the road. They have been assembled from hay and scrap by Jim Bird, a cattle farmer, and his wife Lib. It began when Bird's hay baler churned out some strangely shaped bales; the artist in him saw possibilities and

London Bridge did fall down; then it was shipped to Lake Havasu City and reconstructed.

his marvelous menagerie began to take shape. Lib limits him to a maximum expenditure of five dollars per item. The straw structures are potentially under threat from a proposed highway widening, but the State Historical Commission is already looking on Bird's Follies with some approval. Another locomotive catches the eye up on U.S. Route 23 in New York State, near Windham. A full-size locomotive plus tender and five freight cars is poised to steam across the road. Take a second glance and it's just a pile of firewood, artfully cut, split, and stacked by Alec Alberti, aged nineteen, to attract donations to help pay his way through college.

SPLIT BY HAND
THE FIREWOOD
IN THIS TRAIN
WAS CUT, SPLIT,
AND STACKED
BY
ALEC ALBERTI
AGE 19

THIS IS THE TOOL THAT
SPLIT IT ALL

The Palace of Fine Arts in San Francisco was a focal point in the international 1915 Panama-Pacific Exposition. Designed by Bernard Maybeck in architecture of Bramantean grandeur, it was originally constructed out of plaster and so had a tendency to dissolve in the rain; it was never intended to be permanent. San Franciscans became quite agitated when it finally had to be pulled down in 1962, so much so that in order to placate them a full-size replica of the palace was constructed out of concrete. It now presides in red and ochre majesty over the edge of the Presidio at the foot of the Golden Gate Bridge.

Originally made of rain-soluble plaster, San Francisco's Palace of Fine Arts was recast in concrete in 1962.

When a building is destroyed, most sensible people sweep away the ruins and start over, or use the vacant land for some other purpose. But the beauty and romance to be found in an elegant ruin is undeniable. Piranesi's fame as an engraver lies in his romantic creations of grandiose ruins, magnificent in pen and ink. But in order to create a real ruin great care and thought must be given to the original structure, the donor building. A wooden building can never make a satisfactory ruin. It may look pleasingly threatening as it decays, but rot and mildew will rob it of dignity. No, stone alone makes for a grand ruin. One of the most astonishing sights in Missouri is the skeleton of a house called Windsor, near Port Gibson— a forest of tall, fluted columns with blackened Corinthian capitals supporting the empty sky above them. The "Ruins of Sheldon," near Beaufort, South Carolina, was built in 1745 as the church of Prince William's Parish. The church was burned by the British in 1779, rebuilt in 1826, burned again by Union troops in 1865, and finally left as a ruin. The brick-built columns and arches, shorn of their rendering, make an unforgettable impact in the Carolina woods.

The tradition of the false ruin set in the landscape is a long and honorable one in Europe, inspired by romantic engravers and painters such as Piranesi and Poussin. A young Englishman, Thomas Cole, migrated to America at the age of eighteen in 1819 and was so empassioned by the beauties of the natural scenery that he decided to become a landscape painter. Founding the Hudson River School, he followed the European tradition by enhancing his paintings with picturesque ruins. One of his paintings, *Moonlight,* painted about 1838, is said to have inspired John Church Cruger to re-create ruins for himself on Cruger's Island in the Hudson River, just north of what is now Barrytown, New York. He built a pair of eyecatcher arches about thirty feet tall and adorned them with Mayan artifacts brought from Yucatán by his explorer friend, John Lloyd Stephens, including a Mayan bust and headdress in stone and an intricately carved Kabah door jamb. Cruger liked to take his guests on moonlit boat trips round the island and impress them with his ghostly, romantic ruins and the savage carvings. The ruins, once clearly visible from the river, have decayed and succumbed to the brambles and vines; they have become ruins of ruins. One arch was still standing in the early 1960s, but it fell sometime that decade. The island, now a low-lying peninsula, is not easily accessible and we were unable to check on the present condition of the ruins, but locals say part of a column and a few piles of stones are all that

remain. The Mayan sculptures, unsurprisingly, are no longer there; they can now be seen in the American Museum of Natural History.

With all these wonders punctuating the landscape, a southern slave cabin is an unlikely candidate for inclusion. George W. Johnson, made governor of the Confederate Commonwealth of Kentucky in 1861, was a farmer and lawyer. He built a Greek Revival mansion outside Georgetown, Kentucky, in the rolling pastures of Scott County. The mansion was burned down years ago, but what catches the eye from the distant back road today is not the replacement house, but the pilasters and entablatures of Johnson's slave cabin and smokehouse, extensions of the Greek revival style to buildings usually unconsidered. Was this the gesture of a cruel slavemaster? Johnson was prepared to stand up for his beliefs—he was killed in the Battle of Shiloh in 1862, fighting as a private while still governor, but his slave house is soundly built, a palace among its peers.

What purpose other than to catch the eye can Samuel Colt have had when he added a star-spangled blue onion dome to his gun factory in Hartford, Connecticut, perching it on sixteen columns on an octagonal base, with a six-foot cast-iron horse prancing on the gilded ball finial, the whole ensemble bizarre in the extreme and wonderfully out of context. Colt went through many professional incarnations

The pilasters and entablatures of this slave cabin repeat the Greek revival motifs of the plantation's mansion, long since vanished.

before he emerged as the hugely successful inventor of the Colt revolver: he was a textile worker, a sailor, an entrepreneur (raising enough capital at the age of twenty-two to start his first gun company, which went bust), a chemist, and an inventor (producing a submarine mine and an underwater telegraph). The Colt .45 became known as the Equalizer, from the saying "God didn't make men equal—Sam Colt did." We know that the sixteen-year-old Colt sailed to India, from where the inspiration for his dome may have come. Although his house, Armsmear, built by his nephew H. A. G. Pomeroy, was in the Italianate style, nevertheless it had onion-domed conservatories with gilded finials, now sadly gone. The prancing horse—the colt—has also now disappeared from the factory's dome, and paint is peeling from the drum, a couple of the wooden columns have cracked, but at least it's still there, still the most eyecatching sight in Hartford, the blue, gold, and white Moorish domination of the great drab red brick factory still swivelling heads after 125 years.

And so to sleep, perchance to dream, after another great day's folly hunting across America. Where do we choose to rest our weary heads? There are three eyecatching motels left in America, all concrete wigwams. To be pedantic, they are actually concrete tepees, a wigwam being an Algonquin domed structure while a tepee is a Sioux word for the cone-shaped jobs we normally call wigwams. Confused? You needn't be, for the chances of your being in Holbrook, Arizona, Rialto, California, or Cave City, Kentucky, at the precise time your weary head is pillow bound is remote. These are the last remains of no little plan by architect Frank A. Radford to scatter motels in the shape of tepees across America. He patented the design in 1935 and reasonably quickly allowed seven motor courts, as motels were known in the 1930s, to be built. Cave City's was the first. Radford had a refreshing approach to franchising; he allowed anyone to use his plans on condition that each tepee have a coin-operated radio installed, which played for half an hour for ten cents. He collected his commission in dimes. The Holbrook Wigwam Motel opened in 1950 and closed in 1974, driven out of business by Interstate 40 rushing past the city; in more leisurely days the tepees had been built on the most famous road in America—Route 66. Nostalgia for the old road led to the Holbrook motel being renovated and reopened in 1988. Along with their cousin the TeePee Bar in Lawrence, Kansas, these three are all that remain, enlivened by slogans such as "Do It in a Tee Pee," on the Rialto motel, which is also set on old Route 66 running through a dingy suburb of San Bernadino. The gas station attendant looked at us with horror when we asked directions. "You aren't planning to stay there are you? I wouldn't if I was you."

Frank A. Radford hoped that his concrete tepees would spring up all across America.

Chapter 10

REPLICAS, COPIES, AND THE SEVEN WONDERS OF THE WORLD

The George
Washington
Masonic National
Memorial is a
substantial
building,
although it's
more than a
hundred feet
shorter than its
prototype.

There is a myth that the Great Pyramid at Giza is the only one of the Seven Wonders of the World left standing. Not so. It may be the only one in its original state, but most of the Wonders can be found on a trip through America. Just to refresh your memory, the Seven Wonders are: the Great Pyramids at Giza (built 2600 B.C. and still there after 4,600 years); the Hanging Gardens of Babylon (built 562 B.C. and long gone); the Tomb of King Mausolus at Halicarnassus (built 361 B.C. and demolished ca. A.D. 1500); the Temple of Diana at Ephesus (built 356 B.C. and taken down in the Middle Ages); the Colossus of Rhodes (built 280 B.C. and destroyed by an earthquake less than fifty years later); the statue of Zeus at Olympia (built 430 B.C. and destroyed A.D. 500); and the Pharos at Alexandria (built in 280 B.C. and demolished in the 1300s).

The architect's plans for the Pharos at Alexandria have long been mislaid, but we can get a pretty fair idea of its appearance by looking at the George Washington Masonic National Memorial in Alexandria, Virginia, rather than Alexandria, Egypt. The tower, 333 feet high compared to the 440 feet of the original, consists of three mighty diminishing blocks surmounted by a stepped pyramid, placed above a severe temple base fronted with a Doric heptastyle portico. Its isolation on Shooter's Hill diminishes its size; it is a very

substantial building. Work began on its construction in 1922, and was still carrying on in the 1960s. The architects were Helmle and Corbett of New York City. It is a suitably Pharaonic monument, the pink and gray granite gleaming gold in the setting sun.

What about the first mausoleum, the Tomb of King Mausolus at Halicarnassus? We know what that looked like, because it was demolished as recently as the 16th century to provide building material for the Crusader's castle at Bodrum in Turkey. And if we go to the House of the Temple Scottish Rite of Freemasonry at 16th and S Streets in Washington, D.C., we will find it to be a very passable replica of the Mausoleum, with the addition of guardian sphinxes, superbly built in an authoritative Ionic order in 1910 by John Russell Pope, much more correct than the Grant's Tomb interpretation. The design was based on a conjectural restoration of the Mausoleum made in 1862 by Newton and Pullman. "Freemasonry builds its temples in the hearts of men and among nations" runs the inscription over the entrance to this heavily impressive museum and library.

The Mausoleum of Halicarnassus was reborn at the corner of 16th and S Streets in Washington, D.C.

This Lady Liberty raises her beacon above a warehouse and storage company.

The Colossus of Rhodes was a gigantic statue standing at the mouth of the harbor on the Greek island of Rhodes. Divers keep claiming to have found bits of it on the harbor bed but nothing really remains, so we will just have to imagine what a gigantic statue standing at the mouth of a harbor could possibly have looked like. Or will we? On West 64th Street in New York City there is a statue of a lady holding a flaming torch above her head, standing fifty feet up on the roof of the Liberty Storage and Warehouse Company at number forty-three. The hollow metal statue has an interior staircase leading up to a window at the back of Liberty's head. The photographer is cautioned by a passerby: "That's not the real one, you know." There is another one, uncannily similar, standing on a road junction just outside McRae, Georgia. Now if only there were something like that to greet voyagers sailing into a great port.

The Great Pyramid of Cheops, like the Taj Mahal, is one of the few man-made sights in the world that lives up to its awesome reputation. It is truly immense, but there are much newer, sharper, and cleaner pyramids to be found all over the United States. If you can fight your way through the oceans of recreational vehicles that flood Quartzsite, Arizona, the rock hound's paradise, you may discover a small stone pyramid with a tinplate camel perched on top. This is the Hi Jolly Monument, the tomb of a camel driver who participated in a U.S. Army experiment in 1856 to see how the ships of the desert would fare out west. Things were going well until the Civil War distracted attention from the project; the camels escaped and went native, terrifying the local wildlife and being as obstreperous as only camels can be. There were too few to establish a permanent colony, and the Wild West is now mercifully free from dromedary depredations. Homesick, all the camel drivers shipped home to the Middle East except one, Hadji Ali, who rather took to the Arizona desert and decided to become a prospector. He became a much-loved character in the area, accepting his nickname of Hi Jolly with good grace.

The Luxor Hotel's black glass pyramid is fronted by a ten-story sphinx.

Not far from Quartzsite there is a monstrous black glass pyramid on the outskirts of a strange town in the desert. This is the Luxor in Las Vegas, a 2,526-room, 30-story hotel fronted by a 10-story sphinx, which opened in 1993 and is nearly half as big as the Great

Pyramid, 7,370 miles away. It was built in less than two years, as against twenty for the real thing. The architect was Veldon Simpson, who was also responsible for the monstrous mock medieval Excalibur next door, and the huge MGM Grand, the world's largest hotel, just up the block. Calling his office, I announced I was writing a book on unusual and outstanding American architecture. "Boy, have you got the wrong number!" answered a disaffected employee. I was told of several other pyramids, including one by a Bob Goldsmith and his sons, who apparently built a 90-foot pyramid in Chessfield and put a time capsule inside with photographs and records, but no one seemed to know where Chessfield is.

For the Hanging Gardens of Babylon we simply have to step inside the atrium of any John Portman-designed hotel. The Temple of Diana at Ephesus is reflected in almost every bank and every southern mansion in the country, the classic Greek pediment and columns conveying solidity, security, and respectability. Which is strange, when one considers how few people worship Diana of the Ephesians nowadays. Egyptian gods are equally unfashionable, but there is a bizarre shrine to Akhenaton, the monotheist Pharaoh, taking up an entire block in respectable San Jose, California. Three thousand years of Tel el Amarna, Dendara, Karnak, and Luxor are crammed into one small block containing a museum, a temple, a planetarium, an obelisk, a pylon as propylaeum, an art gallery, and statues to Egyptian gods (including Opet, the rarely seen hippopotamus goddess and mother of Osiris), as well as a bookstore and coffee shop. This is the Rosicrucian Park, a collection of dynastic buildings re-created in 1915 by Harvey Spencer Lewis as the headquarters for his "secret brotherhood," and now a mecca, if such a word should be used, for school parties and tours. There are genuine Egyptian artifacts among the cant and canopic chests, but the link to Tuthmosis III as founder of the Rosicrucians is tenuous to say the least, and the choice of Egyptian architecture should simply be seen as giving pleasure to Mr. Lewis and to us, an oasis of delight to discover in a desert of suburban monotony. One unexpected joy is finding real papyrus growing around the temples. William Hope Harvey's pyramid and obelisk in Monte Ne, Arkansas, now lie somewhere under the waters of Beaver Lake. "Coin" Harvey, financier and sometime financial adviser to Nebraska's most famous son William Jennings Bryan, retired to the Ozarks to compile a permanent record in stone of our dying civilization, but before he could raise all the finance to complete his mighty project, the Great

Depression arrived and left his ruins unfinished. A girls' summer camp took over the remains and and used them as an amphitheater before the Beaver Dam flooded the lot.

The choice of the Leaning Tower of Pisa as an architectural subject is understandable, as are the rash of commercial Leaning Towers of Pizza to be found all over the country. But medieval Tuscany, constantly at war with itself, had another architecture, a grimmer, austere machismo in masonry, that evidenced itself in the building of taller and yet taller towers, stretching the limits of fourteenth-century technology in load-bearing stone. These towers, erected by the feuding Guelph and Ghibelline factions to demonstrate their wealth and power, shared a common heritage, the main point of difference coming in the battlements which were square when Guelphic and notched when Ghibelline. For some reason this style suddenly inflamed passions in the breasts of early twentieth-century Americans and, in the northeast, replicas sprang up like celery. In Watertown, Connecticut, the Republican-American tower is a straight copy (without the Ghibelline battlements) of the Torre del

ARCHITECTURAL FOLLIES IN AMERICA

Mangia in Siena, a mere 245 feet tall compared with the 337 feet of the 1338 original, but because it is in a low-rise area it appears to be even taller. Compare this impression to the George Washington Masonic National Memorial described earlier. There, the memorial's isolation on the top of a steep hill apparently diminishes its size, whereas the Republican-American tower, set on a gentle rise in a hilly city, utterly dominates its surroundings. It is dramatically out of scale with the rest of the newspaper's offices, which were originally designed and built as a railroad station in 1909 by the famous practice of McKim, Mead and White. It is said that the tower was a late addition at the request of the president of the New Haven Railroad. The architects intended its sore-thumb quality to be a rebuke to "meddling amateurs," but such architectural subtleties were generally lost on your average railroad president. He was happy simply to know that his tower was the largest clock tower in New England and one of the largest in the country.

Replicas of Sienese towers—including this one in Watertown, Connecticut—sprang up like celery in early twentieth-century America.

The Ilgair Park YMCA in the Chicago suburb of Niles has the best Leaning Tower of Pisa outside Pisa. It was built in 1932 by industrialist Robert A. Ilg, who was so impressed by the real thing that he erected this half-size copy on his summer estate in Niles, as a water tower to supply his three swimming pools. True American practicality again. Unlike the real thing, Ilg's Leaning Tower, built of concrete and steel instead of marble, was designed to lean, but the Leaning Tower YMCA, which now owns the structure, has decided that it too is unsafe, just like the real one, and access is forbidden.

The Provincetown Tower in Provincetown, Massachusetts, is another variation on the Sienese theme, built to commemorate the first landfall of the Pilgrims in 1620. They waited 280 years before putting up this tower, an image from a strongly Catholic country to mark the arrival of a shipload of Protestants. Still in Massachusetts, in south Boston, another replica of the Torre del Mangia was built, this time for the fire department to dry out their hoses.

The similar tower of the Palazzo Vecchio, the city hall of Florence, inspired the Emerson Bromo-Seltzer Tower in the heart of downtown Baltimore. When they built the original, the Florentines inexplicably omitted to include a revolving 51-foot-tall illuminated bottle of Bromo-Seltzer on the top, but Emerson remedied the shortcoming, and for years it was Baltimore's most notable landmark. The bottle was taken down as dangerous in 1936, but the tower survived, now serving as the Baltimore Arts Center and looking a lot more like the Palazzo Vecchio.

When the Florentines built the Palazzo Vecchio's tower, they inexplicably forgot to put a Bromo-Seltzer bottle on top.

We've already looked at the Taj Mahal in Sausalito and seen both Boldt Castle and the Bok Tower described as America's Taj Mahal. In Atlantic City, New Jersey, stands the antithesis of taste, perfectly targeted at its market: Donald Trump's garish Taj Mahal hotel and casino—striped green, gold, purple, and blue minarets, spires, white and gold onion domes, steeples, and

ARCHITECTURAL FOLLIES IN AMERICA

stone elephants—in an architectural style which, while sometimes referred to as Trump's "billion dollar dream come true," is in fact an outrageous nightmare. It was designed by Francis Dumont, who had never designed a building before in his life. Along the Boardwalk of the Las Vegas of the East you can feast your eyes on a frenzy of kitsch, including a 20-foot-tall white cement reproduction of Michaelangelo's David inside Bally's casino. This slim volume could be packed with nothing but the follies of Las Vegas, Atlantic City, Laughlin, and others, but I'll mention just one more—the blue and purple Isle of Capri Casino in Biloxi, Mississippi. No further comment.

Alliance, Nebraska, is home to Carhenge, a neolithic monument using cars instead of sarsen stones. The Cadillac Ranch in Amarillo, Texas, has a similar concept, but by insisting exclusively on Cadillacs it has a classier feel to it. A more realistic Stonehenge can be found at Maryhill in Washington State. After World War I, Sam Hill, whom we met earlier with the Queen of Romania and the Crown Prince of Belgium, decided to erect a monument to the fallen. The form he chose was Stonehenge, but as that famous monument was in such a sorry state of disrepair after hanging out on Salisbury Plain for 6,000 years, Sam decided to improve it. His stonehenge is complete and finished, set up in a neat tight circle, the way the Druids would have wanted it.

Ali Baba Avenue, Sultan Avenue, Harem Avenue, Caliph Street, Sinbad Street, Aladdin Street, and even Sesame Street lead one to expect a certain style of architecture, and one is not disappointed. Inspired by *The Thousand and One Nights*, the City of Opa-Locka was laid out to the north of Miami in 1925 by the aircraft manufacturer Glenn Curtiss, the town's name being a contraction of the Indian name Opatishawockalocka. What a pity they abbreviated it. The city hall is a Moorish fantasy of domes, minarets, and arches through which the Foreign Legion might charge at any minute. Curtiss wanted to build a model township near his airfield, and he employed the architect Bernhardt Muller to create his dreams. His dreams were Swiss to begin with, then based on the Robin Hood legends before finally settling on the *Arabian Nights*. Outsiders are now discouraged from visiting Opa-Locka; it is not the most salubrious district of Miami. Two policemen in Homestead gave more succinct advice: "Just don't go." I reasoned if I went through quickly enough, I would come to little harm. Opa-Locka was a good idea gone bad; it was pleasantly laid out with streets in great semicircles, the architecture was tacky and fun, but it is now mean and dispirited, tawdry and run down. City hall is really worth seeing, but I didn't feel inclined to linger long. Someone should pump some money into Opa-Locka. It doesn't deserve to die. Over on the west coast in Costa Mesa, California, the Ali Baba Motel, a junior relative of the Opa-Locka City Hall, got itself built in 1972 much to the irritation of the local planning department.

Every country copies the architectural styles of others, whether for fun, homage, or effect. The elaborate Dutch stepped gables, the means by which rich merchants discreetly paraded their wealth in the seventeenth century, were once common motifs in old Nieuw Amsterdam. The Dutch set up colonies in the New World just as enthusiastically as the English, and like them they had their disasters. In 1631, near what is now Lewes, Delaware, a Dutch settlement of twenty-eight men from Hoorn were massacred by the Sikoness Indians. Three centuries later the Delaware state legislature voted to commemorate the tragedy by building a museum, and architect

It's easy to imagine the Foreign Legion charging through the arches of Opa-Locka's city hall.

ARCHITECTURAL FOLLIES IN AMERICA

E. William Martin went to Hoorn for inspiration. He returned half inspired by Hoorn's twin-gabled 1613 town hall, an ideal model for the museum but rather larger than required, so he produced a compromise of Solomonic proportions by simply cutting the town hall in two. The one-gabled Zwaanendael Museum was completed in 1931, a pert Dutch rival to the Victorian ladies of Cape May across the bay.

One of the most remarkable and sustained examples of architectural copying still survives, in a ramshackle condition, in Forest Glen, Maryland, a Washington suburb. Coming around the Capital Beltway in search of this legendary assemblage of every known architectural style, ghostly white steeples tower out of the trees ahead. They have nothing to do with the buildings at Forest Glen; they are the pinnacles of the Washington Temple of the Mormons. Nearby, on the grounds of the National Park Seminary Historic District, are the remains of a remarkable creation. A resort hotel opened here in the woods and gulleys of Rock Creek Park in 1887. Ye Forest Inne, a tumble of towers and half-timbering, sprawling in the quiet woodland, lasted only six years before it failed and the property was bought by John and Vesta Cassedy, proprietors of a girls' school in Norfolk, Virginia. The Cassedys were responsible for creating an astonishing series of buildings on the grounds, intended to educate their young ladies in the architectural, geographical, and historical diversity of the world. As sorority houses scattered around the main building, the Cassedys erected, between 1894 and 1905, a Swiss chalet, an American bungalow, a Spanish mission house, a Japanese pagoda, an English castle, an American colonial house, and a Dutch windmill. This would be remarkable in itself, but every other building in the complex also had a story to tell—an Italian villa as dormitory, an Ionic Greek Revival theater called the Odeon, a French chateau, a Greek grotto, a spectacular gymnasium more like the Parthenon than the Parthenon itself. The Cassedys built relentlessly and inexorably. Perhaps the most curious manifestation of this mania for building (for it must be realized that this was all done from pure building passion—the education of young ladies was a mere excuse) was the plethora of dry bridges, galleries, pergolas, roofed corridors supported by caryatids, covered walkways, and paths weaving across the glen, through the groves, among the buildings; an anthropologist might infer that the young ladies of the seminary were incapable of negotiating stairs and slopes, or else they were allergic to rain. One page in the school

This Japanese pagoda was just one element of the Cassedys' relentless building program.

prospectus proudly featured "A Page Of Bridges," and there they are, winding their double-decked way over nothing more than the forest floor.

All this remains. The Cassedys left after the First World War. The seminary went through two changes of ownership before being compulsorily purchased in 1942 by the United States Army for use as a hospital. It is now an annex of the Walter C. Reed Army Medical Center, and it is in a lamentable state of repair. The world's wealthiest army has let this unique architectural treasure slide into depression and decay, but then armies are not noted as agents of conservation. The place is schizophrenic, a vision of two transparent worlds coexisting in parallel planes, one a living military installation, the other a dead school.

ARCHITECTURAL FOLLIES IN AMERICA

A tour of the property today is an eerie experience. A 1929 map shows that the school had its own railroad station; it also shows, buried behind the boiler house and the stables, the Colored Men's Quarters. Retracing the route you enter the old domain past what is now the Forest Glen Office Building, a rugged Scottish Baronial castle sporting a Spanish hacienda arcade, an utterly confusing mishmash of styles not acknowledged on the school map. Next to this is the Old Post Office with contemporary postcards of the more bizarre National Park Seminary buildings in the window. As you leave you drive over the railroad tracks down Seminary Road. Where the station used to be is now an administration building, and the road winds past it over a bridge—not a Cassedy bridge but a new one, crossing the Capital Beltway—and takes you into the Walter C. Reed Army

The Dutch windmill helped introduce the seminary's young ladies to the architectural diversity of the world.

Grecian yearnings: Above, the once-grand gymnasium is more like the Parthenon than the Parthenon itself; right, this lovely caryatid is from the seminary's Aloha House.

Medical Center Annex. There are evidently people working here, but there is no one to be seen. Incongruously, after the discontinuous 100-year history of the place, a stained glass panel in vibrant colors over the main entrance still reads Ye Forest Inne. The place is decaying and decrepit. The buildings slump dejectedly around. Some, like the Phi Beta Nu sorority clubhouse, the English Castle, are buried beneath rampant vegetation; others such as the once-grand gymnasium are flaking to pieces, a band of red tape limply draped around the great columns of the portico, feebly denying entry for safety reasons. The acroteria on the roof of the music hall have disappeared. Sculptures acquired in Europe after World War I by one of the directors of the seminary still dot the grounds. Everything is rotting in the hot sun, in silence but for the distant hum of traffic from the beltway. For the folly lover this is perfection, the peak moment in the beauty of decay. Refurbished and restored, this characterful assembly would lose its air of mystery and magic, but any further dilapidation and the structures will start to collapse. The buildings must be saved, of course; there is no alternative. There is a vigorous action group, the Friends of Walter Reed at Forest Glen (P.O. Box 8274, Silver Spring, MD 20907), who realize that this collection is unique in America. Now is the time to see it.

Like many of the park's structures, the Odeon theater is in a lamentable state of disrepair.

Chapter 11

BILLBOARD AND ANIMAL ARCHITECTURE

The true folly of buildings such as the Leaning Tower of Niles lies not in their shape or form, but that so much of America's unique heritage has been ignored and left to collapse. Since we met the Leaning Tower of Niles in the previous chapter, it does not belong here; but Charles Kuralt's evocative lament for a vanishing America most certainly does.

Niles, Illinois. The leaning tower of Pisa stands—leans—on Touhy Avenue. I've never known why, but there it is. It enriches the drive down Touhy Avenue. A little north, in Milwaukee, there's a Chinese pagoda gas station. In Florida there's a seashell shop that you enter by walking into the yawning concrete jaws of a giant alligator. These are relics.

I like America's screwball architecture, but it's being replaced everywhere by humorless glass and steel. This is a loss. The interstate highways have done in all those hamburger stands that were shaped like hamburgers; remember them? A historian named Peter H. Smith shares my view. After a few years of commercial archaeology, Mr. Smith says we ought to establish a museum of the American highway to preserve the alligator-jawed gift shops before they're all replaced by carbon-copy modular gas stations. You hardly ever see even a World War II fighter plane sitting atop the roof of a diner any-

ARCHITECTURAL FOLLIES IN AMERICA

more. There used to be squadrons of them. And the Brown Derby in Hollywood—tell me, is it still there in the shape of a big brown derby? And is that papier-mache dinosaur still a gas station in Nebraska? And are they still selling Indian souvenirs out of a two-story concrete tepee in Wyoming? They were last time I passed that way, but America's gaudiest buildings are going fast.

Once the roadside was richer. In the twenties and thirties, if you ran an ice cream stand that wasn't shaped like an Eskimo pie, you couldn't keep up with the competition. Lighthouses, windmills, and giant cowboys beckoned at every mile to the motorist of a slower time. There were hot dog palaces in the shape of hot dogs and car washes in the shape of whales and drive-in movie palaces by the architect of the Taj Mahal. I mean, double arches are nice, but remember those two-story doughnuts on the top of doughnut shops? They have crumbled and we are poorer.

—Charles Kuralt,
Dateline America

Hollywood's world famous Brown Derby restaurant, closed since 1985, was torn down in 1994 after the Northridge earthquake. No other country even comes close when it comes to creating these thrilling structures, drearily known as programmatic architecture. How can such an exciting art form be stifled by such a dull epithet? Robert Venturi called it Big Duck architecture, after the remarkable and famous example on Long Island. Its fame and recognition by one of our leading architects has been its salvation; the duck, now restored, is living in peaceful retirement in a park in Southampton, New York. It was originally built in 1931 by Martin Maurer, the manager of Phillip W. Meyers's duck farm on Route 25 in Riverhead. The essence of such architecture, as I wrote in the introduction, is to attract attention, to make money.

The perfect example is Mammy's Cupboard on U.S. Route 61 just south of Natchez, Mississippi. Even people who have never been to America know of it. It is a brick-built dome, about eighteen feet tall, on top of which is a crude rendering of a black woman in a white blouse holding a tray. It is undeniably eyecatching, a huge black woman in an even huger red crinoline. Henry Gaudit built it as a restaurant in 1940, built it in such an eyecatching fashion that passing motorists simply had to stop and ask, "Hey, what is this?" And having stopped, Gaudit subtly reasoned, they may just as well stay for a coffee or a bite to eat. There is nothing of the folly about this. It is utterly functional architecture, its function being to attract trade.

Billboard architecture has two major manifestations: it either represents a living thing such as a duck, a dinosaur, or a globe artichoke, or a man-made object such as a chest of drawers, a bulldozer, a coffee pot, or a steamship. You will not be unduly surprised by now to learn that all these have at some time formed the basis for buildings. The element of surprise is essential, and it is to be found either in the scale of the object or its location. Whatever or wherever it is, it demands attention.

There is another emotion to be considered here, too: pride, a fine reason for building. Pride is the small town with the biggest loon in the world (it cannot be named here because competition is so fierce that the information will be out of date before publication); shame is the town with the world's second largest ball of twine (Cawker City, Kansas, at the time of writing). What distorted civic pride prompts the erection of such structures? They must realize a rival town would waste little time and much money in building something bigger and better. In 1993 a furniture company in Anniston, Alabama, announced their removal to new premises by erecting a giant chair on the site of their old offices. Intrigued, I looked for more examples—and they were everywhere. Wingdale, New York, claims the World's Largest Chair; Bennington, Vermont, has the World's Tallest Ladderback Chair; Thomasville, North Carolina, boasts the World's Largest Duncan Phyfe Chair, and so on. Who really cares? It's all so gloriously futile. There is an ancient pride in boasting that the biggest must be the best, a pride that can so easily be shattered when it has been bettered. Durant, Oklahoma, had the World's Largest Peanut, but not any more—that honor now goes to Ashburn, Georgia. Murphy, North Carolina, had—perhaps still has—the World's Largest Ten Commandments.

Nursery rhymes have a lot more to answer for than we realized when we enchantingly recited our way through "There was an old woman who lived in a shoe," because there are at least three shoe houses in America, three more than anywhere else in the world, and yes, they all had some commercial connection with shoes. Deschwanden's Shoe Repair, built in 1951 in Bakersfield, California, is just what you'd expect—a shoe repairer based in a large white

ARCHITECTURAL FOLLIES IN AMERICA

shoe. But the palace of shoe houses can be found on U.S. Route 30 in Hellam, Pennsylvania, built in 1948. The Haines Shoe House was for years rather down at the heel, but a recent restoration by Annie Haines Keller, the granddaughter of the original builder, has polished it up no end. Haines built it as a publicity stunt, allowing guests to stay for free. The first year he welcomed elderly couples, the second year newlyweds, but by the third year the novelty had worn thin and he rented the house out. The living room is in the toe, which suffered from subsidence, the kitchen in the heel, two bedrooms in the ankle, and what was an ice-cream parlor in the instep. Ms. Keller and her husband bought the decaying house for $67,500 in 1987. It is now pristine white stucco from head to toe, and it even has a stained glass panel in the front door showing Mahlon N. Haines holding up a shoe in each hand with a sign reading Haines the Shoe Wizard below. And of course it stands on Shoe House Road. I hear there is another shoe house in Storytown, New York, four miles south of Lake George, but without seeing it I can say no more.

Pennsylvanians seem to have been particularly struck by this genre. Further west along U.S. Route 30 is the Koontz Coffee Pot at Bedford, a two-story coffeepot as a roadside diner, and seventeen miles further on is the Grand View Point Hotel at Juniata, wonderfully positioned for a tremendous vista over western Pennsylvania but built, for some inexplicable reason, in the shape of an ocean liner, perched on a hill three-hundred miles from the sea.

The chamber of commerce in High Point, North Carolina, an area known for the manufacturing of fine wood furniture, chose to build its office in the shape of a giant chest of drawers. There is no mistaking the trade of the United Equipment Company in Turlock, California. Its office is built in the shape of a 22-foot-high bulldozer, complete with rocks piled up in front of its dozer blade. The impact is striking and immediate; the company buys, sells, and rents construction equipment. Hiding underneath the bright yellow straight-tilt dozer is a conventional rectangular office, 66 feet by 28 feet; the cab of the dozer acts as the boardroom and the whole construction is made of plywood, except for the caterpillar tracks (the grousers, as we dozer experts call them), which are made of redwood. The idea was conceived by Harold W. Logsdon, the father of the current president, who saw a model of a bulldozer perched on top of a factory in Japan. He came back to California, found a new site by the freeway, and employed local architect Cliff Cheney

There's no mistaking the trade of the United Equipment Company, in Turlock, California.

to realize his dream in 1976. This is a step beyond billboard architecture; a giant coffeepot or donut might trigger ideas of coffee and donuts, but surely few people will drive down the freeway, slap the steering wheel and shout, "Damn! I've gotta get me a dozer this morning!" Wrong. "It's been good for business," admitted Logsdon's son Mitch, "but it gave the highway patrol a real headache to begin with."

The Big Duck may be considerably bigger than the World's Largest Goose, in Sumner, Missouri, but it is not a patch on other more extreme animalistic architecture. Dinosaurs and dragons are probably the most popular creatures to appear as buildings. Their size and our uncertainty as to their morphology allows a degree of creativity on the part of the architect that would not be acceptable if more everyday animals were the models; a goose without a neck would not be recognizable, whereas everybody recognizes a dinosaur. Some Florida examples: there is a 140-foot-long dinosaur at a filling station in Brooksville, very unsatisfactory and crude, like two flat cutouts propped against each other to make a cheap 3-D image. And a tyrannosaurus rex presides over a crazy golf course in

ARCHITECTURAL FOLLIES IN AMERICA

Panama City, and what's more it apparently breathes fire. Most paleontologists agree that the remains of fire-breathing tyrannosaurus rexes have yet to be discovered, whereas dragons are a different matter. The common dragon, *pyrorespirator gallicus*, really does exist, except that nowadays they mostly live elsewhere. The reason nobody has discovered any bones simply proves that none of them have died yet. There is a dragon—sadly not real—at the head of Merritt Island, clearly to be seen from the Eau Gallie causeway. There is one building that is closer to the real thing than any of these. This is a shop in Medicine Bow, Wyoming, that sells rocks, and it is decorated—or largely built—with fossilized dinosaur bones. The right stuff.

America's best dinosaur buildings stand out in the windy California desert at Cabazon. They stand as a couple, much bigger than one expects them to be, a 150-foot-long brontosaurus and a 65-foot-tall tyrannosaurus, the nonfirebreathing species. Claude K. Bell started building them in 1964 at the age of seventy-three. He worked as a modeller for Knott's Berry Farms and for Warner Brothers, building miniature film sets that could then be destroyed by fire, flood, or earthquake, just like the real California. He was still working for Knott's, sculpting figures and running a profitable photo concession when he started building his dinosaurs, and all his spare time was spent building his dream, at a cost of $10,000 a year. The terrible lizards are built on a steel frame, with a concrete skin up to five inches thick, beautifully constructed and rock solid in the howling winds. "When you're doing something like this, you can forget about eating and sleeping, and just live on that tingle of enthusiasm," Bell was quoted as saying. "I've worked all through the night sometimes. A younger man probably couldn't plan this and do it; you need to build up the money, and the dedication, too. When you're young, you're too dumb, you run crazy after girls." His dedication was absolute. He was planning the tyrannosaurus when he was eighty-three. "Why waste time? I plan to work until I cannot. I've got a lot to do before the sand runs out." The tyrannosaurus was completed and the next project was to be a mastodon, but the sands ran out for Claude in September 1988, two weeks before his ninety-second birthday. A lot of people interviewed Claude Bell—the dinosaurs are hard to miss if you drive from Los Angeles to Palm Springs—and he was happy to talk, but at no time could he explain why he built them. Like Simon Rodia, he explained simply that "I wanted to build something big." This is the Rosebud theorem; the

Terrible lizards:
Claude Bell's
tyrannosaurus
(above) and
brontosaurus
(right) are hard to
miss along the
drive from Los
Angeles to Palm
Springs.

ARCHITECTURAL FOLLIES IN AMERICA

passion, from childhood or before, that cannot be expressed in mere words. Where did Bell's passion and inspiration come from? The inspiration goes way back, right back to his childhood in New Jersey, where he used to play on the sands in Margate making models even then, and getting passersby to throw him coins for his work. A little way down the beach was the most wonderful thing the boy had seen in his life, a huge building in the shape of an elephant. "I could do that," he thought. So Margate's lovely, tawdry old Lucy the Elephant is the direct ancestor of Bell's better-built dinosaurs.

Lucy is a six-story elephant with a wooden frame clad in metal, standing by the beach in Margate, New Jersey. She was the brainchild of James V. de P. Lafferty, Jr., a real estate developer from Philadelphia who had bought land in South Atlantic City, as Margate was then known. The lots were uninspiring—low sandy dunes covered with scrub pines and coarse grass, only accessible at low tide. Lafferty was not to be deterred by this unpromising parcel. He hit upon an idea that would simply force people to come to South Atlantic City, and that idea was Lucy. He employed a neighboring architect, William Free, to make sure she stood up, but the patents he prudently took out on his animal architecture were in his own name. Lafferty made no little plans; he included fish and bird forms in his patent application, but in the end he only built elephants. Lucy was not alone. So popular did she become after she was completed in 1881 that she acquired two sisters, one in Cape May and the other on Coney Island in New York. Cape May's "Light of Asia" was built in 1884, a 40-foot-high elephant modeled after Lucy and built not by Lafferty but by James Bradley for the Neptune Land Company. Lafferty had his eye on greater things; that same year work began on the largest piece of animal architecture the world has ever seen, the Colossal Elephant on West Brighton Beach, Coney Island. Twice the height of Lucy, at 125 feet, the Colossal Elephant was intended simply as a tourist attraction. It was seven stories high and had thirty-one rooms. Visitors flocked to see it but not in the quantities Lafferty had hoped. There were now three gigantic elephants to be seen in a 150-mile stretch of coastline, just about saturation level. Lafferty was having financial problems. The patents were not bringing in the required money, and the cost of erecting the Colossal Elephant was too high to provide a reasonable return. In 1887 he sold Lucy to Anthony Gertzen. It was Sophie Gertzen, Anthony's daughter-in-law, who christened the elephant Lucy. Nobody knows why. Newer attractions were drawing visitors away from the Colossal Elephant, and Lafferty sold her to a syndicate to be turned into a boarding house. The last built was the first to go: the Colossal Elephant burned down in September 1896; the Light of Asia, decayed beyond repair, was torn down in 1900; only Lucy, protected by the Gertzens, survived. She became a summer home, then a speakeasy, then the center of a holiday camp. Despite the existence of advertisements for the Elephant Hotel, Lucy was never used as such. The Elephant Hotel was the Turkish Pavilion, which had been erected behind Lucy by Anthony Gertzen. The Gertzen family fortunes lessened over the years, but they gamely clung on to Lucy. By 1970, after years of low maintenance, they could no longer afford to look after the derelict old pachyderm.

Margate's lovely, tawdry old Lucy the Elephant once housed a speakeasy.

Lucy has achieved worldwide fame not simply through her size and bizarre aspect, but through that most popular of soap opera themes: triumph through adversity. We very nearly lost Lucy. The Gertzens had donated the elephant to the City of Margate, but had sold the land to developers. She, therefore, stood in the way of progress, which took the shape of a breathtakingly mediocre apartment block that just had to be built on the lot where Lucy had stood for nearly ninety years. So the Save Lucy Committee was formed, and the rest is a tale of struggles and setbacks, of cooperation and credit. A very shabby old Lucy was slowly towed to her new location on July 20, 1970, and since then the committee has raised more than $750,000 to restore and preserve one of America's most remarkable buildings. At the age of 110, Lucy still has the power to enchant children aged from 1 to 100.

All these animal-inspired buildings share one principle—they were built for humans. Animals themselves barely got a look in, so the author Jack London did something about it. After the international success of his novels *The Call of the Wild* and *White Fang*, London, an avowed socialist, used the money to build a palace for pigs on Beauty Ranch, his estate in Sonoma County, California. The

Each family of pigs had its own living quarters at Jack London's pig palace.

ranch, hidden in the hills above the village of Glen Ellen, is said to be set in one of the Golden State's more beautiful regions, though it is hard to appreciate this through torrential rain. The Pig Palace can certainly be appreciated; it is a fine piece of architecture, designed and built by London himself for his Duroc Jersey hogs. Each family of pigs had its own stall and living quarters in a low-curved structure circling a round central service tower holding grain and ground alfalfa. The structure was complete by 1915, but London died the following year, having proved to his chagrin to be rather more successful as an author than a farmer.

The Prairie Chicken was constructed in 1962 by Herbert Green in Norman, Oklahoma, to demonstrate the synthesis of architecture and environment, a philosophy shared by Paolo Soleri. Both men were taught by Frank Lloyd Wright. Greene constructed his house out of shingle, planks, and corrugated metal, materials intended to reflect the prairie on which it rests, and likened the building to a mother hen protecting her young. It certainly doesn't look like a house. As yet his vision has not been picked up by native Oklahomans with any marked enthusiasm.

One last piece of animal architecture, one final chicken, built not to attract trade or to live in but to amuse children, has recently been completed in Malibu, California, for the Pytka family. Architect William Adams was asked to design a living space for the family's nanny, with a play area below. Adams's axonometric drawings of the finished structure show how its morphology derives piece by piece from the start. It was intended to raise the building above the ground, and the struts designed for that purpose resembled chicken legs. The rest followed: big round eyes, folded wings, beak opening to reveal a staircase hidden inside. It looks much more like an owl, but if they say it's a chicken, then a chicken it is.

Chapter 12

... AND THE REST

This enterprise would fail if all the structures that have caught my eye could be neatly categorized and set out in chapters. They would all be in their rightful places, subject to inspection and analysis, and we could strip away their magic and mystery. So I am delighted there are several examples left over that can't be fitted into any of the artificial constraints I have imposed upon them, including some great places to stay. How does one class Jules' Undersea Lodge, a hotel thirty feet underwater in

At Jules' Undersea Lodge, the wakeup call might be provided by a lobster.

Key Largo, Florida, where I was woken up at four o'clock one morning by a lobster attempting to walk across my window? The Madonna Inn at San Luis Obispo, between Los Angeles and San Francisco, has achieved a certain degree of fame by having each of its rooms decorated in a different style. The motel was opened in 1958 by Alix and Phyllis Madonna, and its prime location ensured its early success. Alix Madonna's fortune came largely from his construction and road building company, an occupation that involved removing hundreds of mighty rocks. Of the various styles of room at the inn, by far the most popular are the rooms decorated as caves—not simply decorated, but created from huge boulders to provide a properly troglodytic environment. No mere showerhead awaits you in the bathroom; the water gushes in a waterfall over a cleft in the rocks, allowing you to feel like the star of a deodorant advertisement. This is not back-to-nature stuff because all civilized amenities are provided, but living in a cave exerts a powerful attraction, for the rooms are booked months in advance. This popularity was not shared by Sidney Stern's Lori Motel in Beatty, Nevada, which had similar thematic rooms, although not on such an outlandish scale. The theme rooms were torn out in 1988 and all that remains is a quiet, orderly motel called the Phoenix Inn, now run by Stern's daughter Susan. The Madonna Inn is unmissable on Highway 101, and the drive between Los Angeles and San Francisco is one of the best in the country; the old Lori Motel is tucked away on a side street in small town Beatty, and few people choose to drive the 443 miles from Reno to Las Vegas for fun. Location, location, location.

The cave rooms at the Madonna Inn aren't just decorated with rocks; they're created from huge boulders.

Chalet Suzanne in Lake Wales, Florida, is famous for its food—I had the best eggs benedict I've ever eaten—but it should be just as renowned for its extraordinarily eclectic architecture. Turrets, gables, towers, balconies, verandas, canopies, anything that pleases the eye has been crammed into the construction of this extraordinary little hotel on the basis that if it's good to look at, it's good to have. The hotel grew organically from its foundation in 1931 by Bertha Hinshaw, and you can see just how it grew. There was a disastrous fire in 1943, but Bertha just picked up and carried on, and the hotel, now run by Bertha's son Carl and his wife Vita, just carried on growing rooms to accommodate the ever-increasing number of guests. It is gradually moving through the Florida countryside like some great powder pink and blue lizard. By the time Arcosanti is finished, Chalet Suzanne should have reached Key West. Part of the grounds is given over to a walled section called the Autograph

Garden. Guests can write messages—"I'm in Love with a Princess! Spot"—on tiles, have them fired in the kiln (the Chalet has its own pottery) and added to the tiled wall. This is serious baby-making territory. Every room is different, horrors to a Sheraton or a Hilton, an absolute delight to guests glazed by L-shaped bedrooms and portion-controlled hospitality. There is only one similar hotel in the world, and that is in the beautiful village of Portmeirion in Wales, which wins on architecture and scenery but loses out on food and hospitality. It also doesn't have its own soup cannery or its own airfield.

In the 1970s the BEST product stores employed S.I.T.E. and James Wines, who wrote a defense of the Big Duck in *Architectural Forum*, to provide a different look for their stores. When the Sacramento, California, store opens for business forty-five tons of brick and masonry at the corner breaks away to reveal the entrance, while at their Houston, Texas, location they have constructed a ruined white brick façade, with a large section tumbling into a random heap on top of the store's canopy. In Hamden, Connecticut, the concept has been extended to a ghost parking lot at the Hamden Plaza Shopping Center on Dixwell Avenue, where it appears that a few automobiles failed to escape the contractor's haste to lay the blacktop. The snout of a Pontiac GTO pokes disgruntledly out of the tarmac.

The location of Curley's Corner was ideal for fishermen who could stop off for bait and a beer on the way from Houston to the Texas coast. Then it was bought by Alan Thayer, a construction company boss who spent twice the purchase price on remodeling the tiny 200-square-foot structure. The old bait store has become a triangular something; even Thayer isn't quite sure what, but it echoes his interest in Central American art. The little building is now adorned with niches, beams, statues of saints, bells, and probably whistles, too. "It has no purpose and, even worse, no parking," complained a local resident. If it puzzles passersby on busy Highway 146, it is only fair that it should puzzle the builder, too.

Where can one find a monument erected to the memory of a left leg lost in battle? What is that field of lightning rods doing in Quemado, New Mexico? What is the secret of the $172 million monument out in the Montana prairie? A giant pair of praying hands rising out of the ground startles passing motorists near Webb City, Missouri. Just imagine the size of the statue they buried there. What drives Jennings and Mitzi Osborne every twelve months to bury their Little

Rock, Arkansas, house in enough red lights to illuminate a midsize town and, feeling they hadn't done enough, buy the houses on either side and light them, too? Why didn't they simply buy Koziar's Christmas Village in Bernville, Pennsylvania? Maybe they already own it. Did you know there is an independent country called Oyotunji within the borders of North Carolina? What does that Gothic folly that Gep Durenberger wouldn't let me see in San Juan Capistrano look like? Does the Cannonball Pyramid still stand in Lemmon, South Dakota? Where is the state of Jefferson?

There is much more out there still to be discovered. America's follies are as diverse and unique as America.

ENVOI

Our revels now are ended. These our actors,
As I foretold you, were all spirits and
Are melted into air, into thin air:
And, like the baseless fabric of this vision,
The cloud capp'd towers, the gorgeous palaces,
The solemn temples, the great globe itself,
Yea all which it inherit, shall dissolve
And, like this insubstantial pageant faded
Leave not a rack behind. We are such stuff
As dreams are made on, and our little life
Is rounded with a sleep.

Shakespeare, The Tempest IV, i
London; Harlech

GAZETTEER

ILLUSTRATIONS

All photographs not specifically credited are by Gwyn Headley.